GREATNESS

THE RISE OF TOM BRADY

BOOK CREDITS

EDITOR: Janice Page
Special thanks to: Gregory H. Lee Jr.

ART DIRECTOR/DESIGNER: Wendy Dabcovich

PHOTO RESEARCHER: Leah Putman
*Additional thanks to: Joseph Sullivan,
Jim Wilson, Lisa Tuite, Steve Pena, Joe Funk*

PHOTO CREDITS

JOHN BOHN: 26, 93, 112

DOMINIC CHAVEZ: 52

BARRY CHIN: 6, 22, 27, 32-33, 41, 50, 82,
86, 96, 107, 113, 123B, 140-141, 149

JIM DAVIS: 1, 5, 8, 35, 37, 39, 43, 44, 46, 48-49,
54, 59, 62, 78B, 82, 83, 85, 87, 89, 92, 93,
104-105, 107, 109, 114, 119, 125, 130,
138 (COVER), 150, 159, BACK COVER

BILL GREENE: 23, 26, 28-29, 57, 129, 155

PAT GREENHOUSE: 31

STAN GROSSFELD: 81, 118, 123, 139, 147

TOM HERDE: 65, 68, 77

JUSTINE HUNT: 132

DAVID KAMERMAN: 121

SUZANNE KREITER: 74

MATHEW J. LEE: 2-3, 8, 10, 53, 69, 78, 96,
101, 143

DAVID L. RYAN: 71, 153

ESSDRAS M. SUAREZ: 145

CHITOSE SUZUKI: 77

JOHN TLUMACKI: 95

JONATHAN WIGGS: 157

BRIAN LANKER /SPORTS ILLUSTRATED: 73

AP PHOTOS: 13, 16, 19, 20, 24, 64

The Boston Globe

This book is available in quantity at special discounts
for your group or organization. For further information,
contact:
Triumph Books
542 S. Dearborn Street
Suite 750
Chicago, Illinois 60605
Phone: (312) 939-3330
Fax: (312) 663-3557
Printed in the United States of America.
ISBN 13: 978-1-57243-842-2

CONTENTS

FROM the TOP

He Rules

by JACKIE MACMULLAN

He is unbeaten, untied, and unequivocally the king of the football world. **Tom Brady may not have been voted the most valuable player of Super Bowl XXXIX, but he is the quarterback of the Super Bowl champion New England Patriots (again), and whenever all the dynasty talk begins in earnest, it starts with the former sixth-round draft choice from Michigan, who has earned his rightful place among Boston legends Bill Russell, Bobby Orr, Larry Bird, and Ted Williams.**

Patriots quarterback Tom Brady has a winning smile, a winning arm, and is a blossoming legend. Is it any wonder that people are after him?

Brady is the money man. He is 9-0 in post-season play. He has a winning smile, a winning arm, and he is a blossoming legend who has cornered the market on storybook endings. How long can this go on? As long as Brady stays healthy, happy, and hungry in a Patriots uniform.

The Patriots are truly a team of champions, but make no mistake: Their remarkable success begins and ends with Brady.

Think about it. For all Bill Belichick's brilliant maneuvers, he was still a coach with a 5-11 record in 2000 and an 0-2 start in 2001 before he entrusted his football team to a young — and unproven — Brady. It has been a magical ride for the quarterback, the team, and the fans of New England. Little boys grow up wanting to wear No. 12 and date Bridget Moynihan. Little girls grow up wanting to be Bridget Moynihan so they can date Brady.

Sometimes, a handsome superstar with charisma, endorsements, and enough press clippings to wallpaper Gillette Stadium encounters jealousy or resentment. Not Brady. He's gone out of his way to be one of the guys, and it's appreciated. Nobody in the Patriots' locker room wants anybody else running the show.

"He's the best quarterback in the game of football," declares linebacker Larry Izzo.

The list of quarterbacks who have won three Super Bowls is very short. Joe Montana. Terry Bradshaw. Troy Aikman. Brady proved he belongs in that hallowed company on a February night in 2005 when he was not his best but, as always, just good enough.

Predictably, the quarterback isn't biting on talk of a dynasty, or his Hall of Fame future. "It's not so much about what we've accomplished in the grand scheme of things, or how it's looked at in terms of history," Brady says. "We're taking them one at a time. We know

how hard it is."

As with most elite players, preparation is a major part of what sets Brady apart. Before Super Bowl XXXIX, safety Rodney Harrison recounted a story of arriving at the practice facility at 6:30 in the morning for the team meetings and seeing Brady covered in sweat.

"He had just finished his workout," Harrison recalls. "While the rest of us were sleeping, he was working on his game."

And when that game was over, the numbers were vintage Brady: 23 of 33 for 236 yards and two touchdowns. Naturally, there were no interceptions.

Tom Brady is only 28 years old. He has a whole football life ahead of him, yet he's already compiled a career of excellence that most players would kill for.

Please don't ask him to put his career in historical perspective. That's our job, not his.

"I love leading this group," he says. "I love calling plays in the huddle. I love being a captain on this team. I see what Dan [Marino] and Steve [Young] have accomplished, and I watched them get into the Hall of Fame, and those guys are unbelievable, because they did it for so long.

"I'd love to play like those guys did. But there's a long way to go."

He has matured, both as a player and a person since that first Super Bowl victory in 2001, which seems like decades ago. Back then, the Patriots shocked the world. Now the only way they shock the world is if they lose.

Brady wouldn't know about that. He does not lose. Not in the big games. Not in the Super Bowl.

Maybe it won't last forever. Let him worry about that some other day. Right now, it can't get any better. Right now, the quarterback of the New England Patriots is king. ◆

> ## Tom Brady is only 28 years old ...yet he's already compiled a career that most players would kill for.

STEADY AT THE HELM

Tom Brady is tied with Bart Starr for most consecutive postseason wins by a starting quarterback.

WINS	PLAYER	TEAM	YEAR	TITLES	COMP	ATT	PCT	YDS	TD	INT	RTNG
9	Bart Starr	Packers	1961-68	*5	109	179	60.9	1,575	14	3	108.5
9	Tom Brady	Patriots	2001-05	3	190	304	62.5	1,951	11	3	88.7
7	Terry Bradshaw	Steelers	1974-76	2	75	125	60.0	1185	9	6	95.5
7	Joe Montana	49ers	1988-90	2	143	204	70.1	1,897	20	2	127.8
7	Troy Aikman	Cowboys	1992-94	2	145	201	72.1	1,818	16	4	118.0
7	John Elway	Broncos	1997-98	2	96	182	52.7	1417	6	3	82.8

* includes 1961, '62, and '65 NFL championships, along with Super Bowls I and II.

When you've won as much as this quarterback has, victory expressions are routine.
He may be young, but Brady is already keeping some elite company.

BRADY'S FOURTH-QUARTER COMEBACKS

In his first four seasons as an NFL starting quarterback, he led the Patriots to victory 17 times when facing a tie or deficit in the fourth quarter, including all three Super Bowl victories.

	DATE	OPPONENT	SCORE	TIME LEFT	ATT	COM	YDS	TD	INT	FINAL
	Oct. 14, 2001	San Diego	16-26	8:48	18	13	130	1	0	* 29-26
	Dec. 2, 2001	at NY Jets	14-16	15:00	7	6	56	0	0	17-16
	Dec. 16, 2001	at Buffalo	6-9	5:57	13	9	116	0	0	* 12-9
p	Jan. 19, 2002	Oakland	3-13	15:00	27	20	138	0	0	* 16-13
s	Feb. 3, 2002	St. Louis	17-17	1:30	8	5	53	0	0	20-17
	Sept. 22, 2002	Kansas City	38-38	0:00	5	4	46	0	0	* 41-38
	Nov. 10, 2002	at Chicago	19-30	5:22	14	9	116	2	0	33-30
	Dec. 29, 2002	Miami	13-24	4:59	13	8	69	1	0	* 27-24
	Oct. 5, 2003	Tennessee	24-27	4:40	1	1	15	0	0	38-30
	Oct. 19, 2003	at Miami	13-13	15:00	10	7	147	1	0	* 19-13
	Nov. 3, 2003	at Denver	23-26	2:51	5	4	58	1	0	30-26
	Nov. 23, 2003	at Houston	13-20	3:11	14	10	133	1	0	* 23-20
	Nov. 30, 2003	at Indianapolis	31-31	10:21	6	3	31	1	0	38-34
p	Jan. 10, 2004	Tennessee	14-14	15:00	11	6	27	0	0	17-14
s	Feb. 1, 2004	Carolina	29-29	1:08	5	4	47	0	0	32-29
	Oct. 3, 2004	at Buffalo	17-17	15:00	4	2	8	1	0	31-17
s	Feb. 6, 2005	Philadelphia	14-14	15:00	4	2	33	0	0	24-21

p-divisional playoff; **s**-Super Bowl; *overtime

EARLY YEARS

Humble Beginnings

by JIM MCCABE

January 18, 2002 | When, as it often does, the fog settles in over the San Francisco Peninsula, it is a gray soup, thick and lingering, and you are challenged to distinguish between myth and legend.

It turns out cable cars may not exactly climb halfway to the stars. An imprisoned Birdman is ancient history. And you can forget the shroud of mystery around a young quarterback who has folks back east scratching their heads in wonderment.

Tom Brady? No surprise to a legion of supporters here, all of whom will flash smiles as wide as the San Mateo Bridge that stretches over the south end of San Francisco Bay, then tell you that he's always been special.

Granted, the onetime star at San Mateo's Junipero Serra High School never was labeled a "can't miss talent" complete with eye-popping numbers, but if you were able to look beyond such superficial layers, there was no mistaking the intangibles — his heart, his push to excel, his commitment. He's the kid, after all, who came up with a jump-roping drill that so impressed the high school coach it was made part of the training regimen.

Brady's supporters never questioned his talent; only if and when the NFL chance would ever present itself. But even these people were stunned by the swiftness with which this fairy

San Mateo is a long way from Ann Arbor, where this Wolverine cut his teeth while learning how to hand off gracefully. Here he orchestrates a 1998 win against Michigan State.

tale has unfolded — from sixth-round draft pick in 2000 to fourth-string quarterback in early 2001 to Pro Bowl leader of a divisional champ a few months later. All of which has Tom Martinez raising a toast to a student who has truly seized upon an opportunity, though he is careful to give proper thanks where it belongs: "God bless Bill Belichick. I'm not sure if the Patriots coach were offensive-minded whether Tom would have gotten the chance, but Belichick obviously believes in him, and I have so much respect for him because of that."

The first step on this magical ride was Brady's debut as a starter, Week 3 in Indianapolis, a 44-13 triumph, after which he signed a game ball and sent it to Martinez.

"It shows you what kind of person he is," said the longtime football coach at the College of San Mateo who is a sort of quarterback guru in these parts. His summer camp for quarterbacks and receivers is a must for aspiring players in the Bay Area.

"I always said you have two ears and one mouth, so you should listen twice as much as you talk," said Martinez. "But so many young kids don't want to listen. Tommy did. We'd sit, I'd talk, he'd listen, then he'd go and work at it. He worked his ass off and always believed in himself."

And now, believers from New England and around the NFL are lining up, too. Of course, you'll find 'em toward the back, behind all those folks who were won over by Tom Brady long before he landed in Foxborough.

Junipero Serra High School sits just off of Route 92, lodged in a neighborhood of modest-sized homes — albeit with million-dollar prices — that is bordered on one side by the swank Peninsula Country Club and on the other by El Camino Real, which cuts through downtown San Mateo.

> "So many young kids don't want to listen. Tommy did."

"I was a 49ers fan... I didn't pay too much attention to [the Raiders]," Brady said. "They were on the other side of the Bay."

Located between San Francisco and San Jose, the all-boys Catholic school was named after Padre Junipero Serra, the Franciscan who introduced Catholicism to California in the 1700s.

Conscious of its religious heritage, the school is also proud of its athletic glory, particularly in baseball, where nearly two dozen graduates have gone on to play professionally, including Jim Fregosi, Gregg Jefferies, the late Dan Frisella, and a fellow named Bonds: Barry Bonds.

In football, John Robinson played here, as did the incomparable Lynn Swann. Pete Jensen, Brady's high school baseball coach, can't help but bubble over with pride when he says, "It's been a great year for Serra. Swann was inducted into the Hall of Fame, Bonds hit 73 home runs, and now Tom Brady."

Indeed, the youngest of Thomas and Galynn Brady's four children, the one (born Aug. 3, 1977) who never played football until ninth grade — and even then he was a backup linebacker because he was pudgy enough to mandate the position —has got the locals thinking about another football team other than the 49ers and Raiders.

"Thank goodness for DirecTV," said Steve Loerke, Brady's longtime friend and former Serra teammate. He and Kevin Brady (no relation), who was a baseball teammate of Tom Brady's, host friends every Sunday in their townhouse just south of San Mateo, and the Patriots games are the featured attraction.

"Tom's defeated all the odds, if you look at everything that's happened to him," said Loerke, a financial consultant who cuts short many summer workdays to run routes and catch footballs from his old friend. "If there was one word I'd use to describe him, it'd be perseverance."

14

No one seems to dispute that description. Not his high school teammates. Not his coaches or teachers at Serra. Not his college coaches at Michigan. In fact, none of them would blame Brady if at times he felt like one of those inflatable toys — the kind you can punch and push, because you know it will just bounce right back.

"I remember calling him into my office, right after his junior season [in 1993]," said Tom MacKenzie, Brady's high school football coach. "I told him that the coaching staff had decided not to nominate him for All-League. We could have, because his stats said yes. But we said no."

Why?

"Because we knew he was capable of doing better. And we wanted to get across the message that things in life are earned, not given."

MacKenzie concedes it was a rough way to send a message to a teenager and that "we took a risk as a coaching staff," but in Brady they saw something they rarely see in young players.

"He's confident, but not arrogant. He believes in himself, but it's not cockiness. He didn't moan when I told him. That's been his history."

Friends say if that decision hurt, Brady never let on. And it perhaps explains why, six years later, he didn't stir things up when the Michigan staff defied logic with a decision that could have ignited a firestorm of controversy. Though as a junior he had completed 61.1 percent of his passes (214 of 350) for 2,636 yards and 15 touchdowns in Michigan's 10-3 campaign in 1998, Brady received a jolt to start his senior season: In a precursor to what has happened this year, he found himself involved in a playing debate against a crowd favorite named Drew — in this case Drew Henson, the local hero from Brighton, Mich.

A sophomore with heralded skills, Henson was toying with the idea of signing with the New York Yankees (in fact, he would leave Michigan in his junior year to play baseball

full time), so observers openly wondered if giving him playing time wasn't a veiled attempt to win him over to football. Nonsense, said coach Lloyd Carr, who insisted it was the only way to have an experienced backup. Either way, the end result was definitely unconventional — Brady would start the game, Henson would play the second quarter, and at halftime the coaches would decide which of them played the second half.

On paper, it seemed a recipe for disaster, but Michigan coaches contend it wasn't — thanks to Brady.

"The way we presented it, I think he trusted us," said Mike DeBord, then Michigan's offensive coordinator. "I'm not saying he did or didn't like it, yet Tom Brady never flinched, never complained. He took a difficult situation and handled it beautifully."

"Nothing was ever given to him," said Stan Parrish, then the quarterbacks coach. "He earned everything he got."

The first five weeks Brady earned the coach's nod to settle in as the second-half starter, but then came the game at Michigan State. Henson started after halftime, threw a costly interception, and Carr was forced to call upon Brady late in the game. From a 27-10 hole, he nearly rallied the Wolverines, but a 34-31 defeat was the team's first of the year. Brady completed 30 of 41 passes for 285 yards and a pair of touchdowns. He split the duties for one more game (another loss to Illinois) before the experiment was deemed over. Brady, once again the team's full-time quarterback, led Michigan to five straight wins to close out the campaign at 10-2.

"In my opinion, that was a huge turning point in his career," said Martinez. "I mean, the way he handled it was to go out and play well and not get caught up in it."

Certainly, if you accept the notion that Henson was thrown at him as a gauntlet, Brady responded in a fashion that doesn't surprise his supporters. "That's the thing that always impressed me about Tom," said DeBord. "He

never backed down from a challenge." The final act in his brilliant collegiate career came in the glare of the Orange Bowl, against a strong Alabama team. Brady put on a show, finishing with 34 completions in 46 attempts, good for 369 yards, 4 touchdowns, and a 35-34 victory. DeBord, who had already decided to leave Ann Arbor for Central Michigan University, searched out his quarterback at the game's conclusion for an emotional embrace.

"I told him if I had to be leaving Michigan, I was glad I was leaving with Tom Brady. That's not putting down any of the other Michigan quarterbacks, because there were some great ones; it's just putting him on another pedestal."

WILLING TO WORK

To casual observers, quarterbacks are judged by numbers, which explains why Brady didn't set the world on fire during his two varsity years at Serra. The teams went 6-4 and 5-5 and Brady completed 219 passes for 3,514 yards in those 20 games. Modest numbers, especially when compared with California's top quarterback in 1994, Kevin Feterik of Los Alamitos, who had more than 3,000 yards in his senior year alone and went on to Brigham Young. In fact, Brady doesn't hold any school records: The Serra marks are shared by the Freitas brothers, Jesse (who later played for the Chargers) and Jim.

There were some real lowlights, too. Like 66-6 and 44-0. Those were the back-to-back defeats Brady and Serra absorbed in his junior year. Or his final two games as a senior, when victories would have propelled the Padres into the Central Coast Section playoffs. Brady completed just 13 of 41 passes for 188 yards in the two games as Serra got beat, 12-0 and 27-6.

"We look back now and wonder, how did we not win?," said Matt Buzzell, an offensive lineman and linebacker on those Serra teams, and a longtime friend of Brady's. "It was disappointing."

MacKenzie concurs. So do Loerke and Giovanni Toccagino, perhaps Brady's favorite target those years. But while the team may not have played to its potential, the blame did not rest with the kid taking the snaps, even though it's forever football to point fingers at the QB. MacKenzie built his team around Brady, a dangerous blueprint when young high school egos are involved, and in doing so he concedes he may have created tension.

"There were a number of guys upset over the notoriety he was receiving, a typical high school jealousy thing," said Loerke, "but I remember being in the huddle, Tom had such control. Win, lose, or draw, you knew you had a friend in Tom who commanded your respect."

For good reason, said Toccagino.

"He was very dedicated and worked his ass off. I remember we used to do this drill, five dots we called it. It was to improve your foot work and man, we hated it." Players would count their blessings when practice was over, for it meant no more "five dots." So imagine Toccagino's shock one day when he wandered over to Brady's house, just a few blocks from Serra. "I couldn't believe it — he had set up the drill at his house. He was doing it at home. I'll never forget that, but that's what he was always about: trying to do something better."

Brady's family house on Portola Drive, a mere five-minute walk to Freitas Field behind the high school, was a popular hangout for his friends, with video games their main source of entertainment. No part-time jobs for Brady, because he "worked at working out, three, four hours every day," said Loerke, who would

Brady fires one of 30 passes (17 completions, 224 yards, two touchdowns) during a 1998 trouncing of Penn State, 27-0.

join his friend for long sessions at the Pacific Athletic Club in Redwood, a place that was frequented by names such as Jerry Rice and Tom Rathman.

Always, said MacKenzie, Brady was motivated by what he truly believed: "It's not what people think you can do, it's what you do."

And what he did was absorb the principals of quarterbacking as taught by Martinez, a guy who didn't care a lick about piling up numbers. "I teach mechanics," said Martinez. "Technique. And what I see is that most kids don't have technique. But if you watch Tom, I'm not saying he's the best in the NFL, but mechanically he's very good. He stays in the pocket, throws it within the frame of the guy catching it, points his front shoulder where he's throwing it, and he throws it overhand."

From summer camp to a 7-on-7 passing tournament to more summer camps, Brady put his grasp of the basics on display, opening eyes as he went along. How he performed for Serra was important, but Martinez said college and pro scouts put more stock in the summer camps. When he was named MVP at the prestigious camp at the University of California, Brady had set the offers in motion.

Southern Cal, UCLA, Colorado, Oregon, Texas A&M, and Illinois were hot in pursuit. Perhaps sensing that a Big Ten rival was going to land Brady, Michigan entered the picture and he agreed to include Ann Arbor among his five allotted visits. Not that many people thought it mattered, because the assumption was the West Coast kid would stay home — just across San Francisco Bay, in fact, at the University of California.

Division 1. Pac-10. Close to his family and friends. It all seemed so perfect, so logical. Right? Well, no. Not if you knew Brady the

way his friends did. "I think he was thinking outside the box," said Kevin Brady. "Looking for the biggest challenge."

Certainly, that was Michigan, for Brady would compete against four or five other quarterbacks in camp, at a place that was drenched in aura, with a 100,000-seat stadium, and decades of great history.

"Michigan is one of those great places," said Keith Gilbertson, then the head coach at California who wanted Brady badly. "He was our No. 1 guy, the key to our whole recruiting class. It was a real blow to us, quite a loss."

Brady phoned Gilbertson to tell of his selection, offering apologies and best wishes. He never sought out MacKenzie's opinion, nor Martinez's, and while he confided in his father, the choice was his. An explanation was perhaps contained beneath his senior class yearbook photo, where Brady wrote: "If you want to play with the big boys, you gotta learn to play in the tall grass."

CHOOSING FOOTBALL

Well before the 1993 Junipero Serra High School football season, the Brady name was known in San Mateo, thanks to Maureen, Tom's oldest sister and a softball legend of sorts. She set a state record for strikeouts and another mark for perfect games (14). There was a 32-1 record one year, and at Fresno State she was an All-American who led the nation in wins (36) as a junior. Right behind her, Julie and Nancy carried on the tradition as outstanding softball players, and Galynn (tennis) and Tom Sr. (golf) are accomplished in their sports, so you could say Tom Jr. simply followed right along.

Thus, it was no surprise when the pro scouts came calling. In baseball, that is.

"He was a definite prospect," said longtime scout Gary Hughes, who has worked for a

> "It was in his nature to compete, even in the classroom."

With three big sisters, the quarterback has never lacked fans. No wonder he says family is one of his favorite things to talk about.

number of major league teams (Florida back then) and is the man who signed John Elway for the Yankees. "A big catcher, and sometimes you shy away from big catchers, but he was projected as a power hitter with a very good arm who handled pitchers well."

Brady was selected by the Expos (post-Dan Duquette, in case you're wondering) in the 18th round, but that is not a true representation of his potential, according to Jensen. The Serra coach also scouted for the Mariners back then and got a thrill out of watching Brady hit four out of the park in a tryout at the Kingdome, but there was never a thought about exercising leverage.

"The thing was, Tom and his father were extremely honest with the [baseball] scouts," said Jensen. "They were pursuing football and they said so, which is why he went late. He was a first- or second-round pick. In fact, the Expos offered him first- or second-round money, but he was going to Michigan for football."

After red-shirting, Brady barely played as a freshman (two games in mop-up, 3 of 5 for 26 yards and 1 interception). And while Brady is remembered for his junior and senior campaigns, DeBord is quick to point out what he did as a sophomore, in 1997.

"It went down to the wire — who were we going to play: Brady or [Brian] Griese?" said DeBord. "Tom put up a great challenge."

BRADY'S YEARS AT MICHIGAN

YEAR	1996	1997	1998	1999
REC	8-4	12-0	10-3	10-2
G	2	4	13	12
ATT	5	15	350	341
COMP	3	12	214	214
PCT	60.0	80.0	61.1	62.8
YDS	26	103	2,636	2,586
TD	0	0	15	20
INT	1	0	12	6
LONG	13	26	76	57

A 27-yard touchdown pass flies off to receiver David Terrell with 58 seconds remaining in the first half of 2000's dramatic Orange Bowl matchup against Alabama. Final score in overtime: Michigan 35, 'Bama 34.

In the end, Carr went with Griese, who led the Wolverines to their first national championship in 49 years. Great for Michigan, though it made for a tough act to follow the next year when Brady assumed command. There wasn't a national championship, but DeBord emphasizes that in the 25 games Brady started, Michigan went 20-5.

"I'm not surprised at what he's done, not at all. And I'm not just saying that," said DeBord, who knows Brady's stock dropped because of the unconventional rotation with Henson. To plenty of NFL scouts, it sent up a red flag — there obviously was something wrong with the kid, they assumed.

"Poor build, very skinny and narrow." "Lacks great physical stature and strength." "Lacks a really strong arm." Those were just some of the comments made by the critics, but none of them ever talked to Jensen or Jesse Freitas, who played in the old All-America Football Conference before settling in as a legendary coach at Serra, where his two sons were star players.

Jensen teaches architecture and Jesse Freitas used to teach geometry, subjects that require precision and attention to detail, and Brady brought his passion into the classroom. "He was all business in the classroom and paid attention to details, which you have to do with geometry," said Freitas, for whom the Serra field is named. Adds Jensen: "It was in his nature to compete, even in the classroom."

The Patriots were one of the few teams not scared off. When Belichick came into control in January 2000, he felt he needed another quarterback on the roster and he ordered then-quarterbacks coach Dick Rehbein to scout the draft. Rehbein — who tragically died just before the start of the 2001 season — offered two candidates, but Brady was the

> "I'm excited when we win games — individual stuff never meant a lot to me."

one he liked best. Rehbein and, later, Belichick were impressed by Brady's accuracy (62.3 percent completion rate at Michigan), his leadership, and the fact he didn't turn the ball over (20 touchdowns to 6 interceptions in his senior year).

No. 10 for Michigan became No. 199 in the 2000 NFL Draft, the sixth quarterback chosen in a year when that position was weak. Brady, so far as most people were concerned, was not much more than an afterthought.

The Patriots had Drew Bledsoe, a franchise quarterback if ever there was one, and the intriguing Michael Bishop. In the middle of those spectrums were veteran backups — John Friesz in 2000, Damon Huard in 2001. It was a mix that left Brady off in the wings — and under the wing of Rehbein, who nurtured the young quarterback.

Far from public viewing, perhaps, but apparently close enough to catch Belichick's attention.

"People questioned us keeping four quarterbacks last year," Belichick recalled during the 2001 season. "Tom wasn't really ready, but he showed us enough and we wanted to work with him.

This didn't happen overnight. It's been a lot of hard work." Call it the joining of a no-nonsense, low-risk quarterback with a no-nonsense, low-risk coach.

"He's perfect for Belichick," said Martinez. "There are more talented guys, yeah, but he doesn't get you in trouble and he sort of wears on you. And he's so damn humble."

"I'm excited when we win games — individual stuff never meant a lot to me," Brady said as he prepared for his first NFL playoff game, against the Raiders at Foxboro Stadium. "We're in the playoffs. It's a big step for a team. It's not about my next step; it's about our next steps."

As a pro, Brady still demonstrates the same practice-makes-perfect work ethic he was known for in high school and college.

The experience with Henson has come in handy, said friends, because Brady respects Bledsoe and has seen quarterback dilemmas from both sides — the starter in danger of being replaced and the backup replacing the starter. He avoids drawing attention to himself. That's how he's always been.

"I tell you, some people are born into it, others work for it," said Martinez. "Tom's an example of someone who had a dream, like we all do. Only he went and did something to make his dream come true."

The autographed football is a proud reminder of Martinez's contributions, and down the road at Junipero Serra High School, MacKenzie nods to a blank spot on his office wall where he plans to put his reminder.

"All I want is an autographed action photo of Tom, so I can point to it and tell kids, 'There's a guy who did it the right way.'" ♦

Mysterious Draft

by BOB RYAN

November 6, 2001

Sixth round? Sixth round?

Are they all dummies, the Patriots included? Every team in the league had multiple opportunities to make Tom Brady one of their own. Even the Green Bays and Philadelphias and others who are quite properly in love with their incumbent starting quarterbacks are always on the lookout for a quality backup. So why was Brady the 199th man chosen, instead of, say, the 89th, or 41st, or 18th, or even higher? He sure is playing like a No. 1 pick.

"It was the way Michigan handled him," said Patriots coach Bill Belichick. "There wasn't a whole lot to go on. He was splitting time with a freshman [Drew Henson]."

Really? The book shows that during his junior and senior years at Michigan, Brady started 25 of 25 games and threw 710 passes. That's more than 27 a game. He had to be logging some pretty serious playing time. He aired it out a school-record 56 times against the dastardly Buckeyes of Ohio State (completing a school-record 31 for a school-record 375 yards).

As a senior, Brady threw 20 TD passes, as opposed to six interceptions. Only Elvis Grbac (21 in 1990 and 25 in '91) threw more TDs in a season for the Wolverines and only Jim Harbaugh ever threw for more than the 2,636 yards Brady rang up in 1998.

Whatever. The coach has it in his head that Brady was being somewhat neglected at Michigan. That's his story, and he's sticking to it.

"If you're not starting in college," Belichick said, "what's going to make you think he's

Michigan quarterbacks meet the media in 1999. (Pssst! Watch the guy on the right.)

going to come in and save your franchise?"

Belichick and the Patriots weren't alone. The entire league passed on him through five full rounds and into the sixth. And it wasn't as if he were playing in some maligned or forlorn program. He was playing before 100,000 people, not to mention every scout, player personnel director, and general manager known to mankind. Michigan football isn't exactly a secret. And the wise men all decided that Brady wasn't much of a prospect. C'mon, the sixth round is the sixth round.

(This is probably as good a time as any to remind you that this is the same league that gave you Jeff George, a.k.a. the Combine Kid. In the modern NFL, throwing a football through a tire at 40 paces often has more resonance than putting actual living and breathing football teams into the end zone.)

SIXTH-ROUND GEMS | A look at some other significant sixth-round catches in recent years.

PLAYER	POSITION	YEAR	PICK	COLLEGE	TEAM
Marc Bulger	QB	2000	168th	West Virginia	New Orleans
Has twice passed for over 3,800 yards for the Rams					
Mike Anderson	RB	2000	189th	Utah	Denver
NFL offensive Rookie of the Year with 1,487 yards					
Matt Hasselbeck	QB	1998	187th	BC	Green Bay
Seahawks dealt first-rounder to make him 2001 starter					
Matt Birk	T	1998	173rd	Harvard	Minnesota
Made 2000 Pro Bowl in first season as starter					
Dusty Zeigler	C	1996	202d	Notre Dame	Buffalo
A Pro Bowl alternate in 2000					
Terrell Davis	RB	1995	196th	Georgia	Denver
Led AFC in rushing 1996-1998; named MVP in 1998					
Willie Williams	CB	1993	162d	W. Carolina	Pittsburgh
Led AFC with 7 interceptions in 1995					

Listening to Belichick rhapsodize about Brady now makes you wonder what scouts and GMs were looking at two years ago. "One of Tom's strengths is his ability to handle things that aren't scripted," Belichick said.

"There are times when you should hold onto the ball a count or two longer in order to allow a play to develop, and he can do that. There are times when you've got to hold onto the ball in order to avoid being strip-sacked, and he does that, too. Some guys never learn [Rob Johnson?]." Belichick cited other subtle aspects of quarterbacking, such as time management, and says that Brady has a firm grasp of these, too. All those scouts and pooh-bahs couldn't see this? Apparently not.

OK, there's more to the story.

"Brady is a lot better now," Belichick said. "He was a skinny 205-pound kid when he came here. He looked as if he'd get killed back there, and he might have been. What the fans and the media don't see is how much hard work he has put into all this. He's got 15 additional pounds of muscle. His mechanics are so much better. There were flaws in his delivery that he's corrected. He's definitely better. He's deposited this in the bank and he's earned some interest."

The mentor also says that the time is right for Brady to flourish. "If Brady had been put in this situation last year, playing for that team, everyone would say, 'What's he doing out there?' and they probably would have been right," Belichick said. "This isn't 1999, and this isn't Michigan, either." As far as scouting in general is concerned, and how a Brady could slide and slide and slide, Belichick said teams always have a lot of self-doubt. If, for example, they like a player no one else seems to have an interest in, it does set off a warning buzzer.

> "This isn't 1999, and this isn't Michigan, either."

"When you're after a player no one else is after, you say to yourself, 'What are we missing?'" Belichick said. "You don't want to follow the crowd, but you've got to take a look. That's scouting. But there's no question: If you're on a guy and nobody else is, you've got to throw up the flag."

In this particular case, Belichick & Co. claim they were spooked by Michigan's interest in playing Henson when they still had Brady; at least, that's the way the coach remembers it.

The Patriots just figured Michigan must have known something they didn't. Either that, or both players in question were simply tremendous prospects, a la Barry Sanders and Thurman Thomas at Oklahoma State, or, going way back, King Hill and Frank Ryan at Rice. That possibility, Belichick says, is remote. But they did take Brady, however late.

They now appear to have two quality quarterbacks heading for some kind of signal-calling collision, and if you think the coach is going to put his hand on that particular conversational stove, get real. "I'm only trying to beat Buffalo," he said. "Brady gets to start against Buffalo, and that's where we're at."

That there possibly could be an issue when one guy goes first in the draft and makes umpty-zillion dollars and the other guy goes 199th and is practically clipping coupons tells you one thing for sure: The men who call the shots in the NFL may work hard at their craft, but none of them is a whole lot smarter than you, Mel Kiper Jr. or my mailman. Tom Brady is proof of that. ♦

Stats don't always measure heart or predict aptitude. Maybe that's why so many so-called experts missed this diamond in the rough.

2000 SEASON

First Shot

by JIM GREENIDGE

December 5, 2000 | It was the first time Patriots rookie quarterback Tom Brady had seen game action—the Patriots' last series of a 34-9 loss to Detroit at the Silverdome Thanksgiving Day. Brady completed one of three passes for 6 yards.

"I didn't make a big deal out of it at all," said Brady, who was inactive again for last night's game against Kansas City. "Obviously, it's a lot of fun to be in there, but it's hardly anything, really." Regardless of his position on the depth chart, Brady, a sixth-round draft pick out of Michigan, prepares the same way every week.

"You've got to prepare each week like you're going to be No. 1 and if you do that, you know you're ready no matter where you're at," he said. "That's the approach I've taken the whole season. I always prepare like I'm going to be in there, and the coach tells me whether I'm dressing this week. There were times I didn't dress, but at least I was prepared. You never know what's going to happen."

Brady was inactive for nine games before dressing as the third-string (or emergency) quarterback at Cleveland Nov. 12. Brady has seen it all in practice, however. He's been versed in multiple defenses and an assortment of blitz packages.

Brady has become somewhat of a film student, as well. The rookie routinely spends several hours each week watching tapes

Kid Patriot at rookie minicamp.

of upcoming opponents. "You need to see things happen before they actually do and you have to make quicker decisions," Brady said. "I've got to continue to improve, to be on top of things."

His preparation is also about getting himself stronger and faster. A two-year starter in college, Brady's weight has jumped from 200 pounds last season to 210 through weight-lifting. He wants to add 10 more pounds.

"My legs are now a lot stronger, so you're able to take the hit more and you're able to make throws now after guys hit you."

Brady said there is no comparison between college football and the NFL. "It's much more intense and things change from week to week [in the NFL]," Brady said. "There are fewer guys on the team, there's not as much practice time, so there are definitely a lot of differences."

Most weeks, Brady runs the scout team workouts and spends little time with the first team.

"You try to take as many mental reps as you can, watching the guys, watching how the older guys do it," he said. "And when you do get your chance, you try to assimilate some of the plays you're running with your offense, paying attention in the meeting room and staying out there and working with guys in similar situations."

With Drew Bledsoe bothered by an injured right thumb for several weeks, Brady has been getting more snaps with the starters.

"It's a comfort zone you've got to get into. The more you're out there, the more you're playing, the more comfortable you'll be out there," Brady said. "I'm starting to be more comfortable out there.

"You draw on the experience that you've had in the past. Obviously, when you don't get as many repetitions in practice, you've got to draw on past experience and past plays, stuff that you're used to that you can draw from when you need to."

Whether it means getting in early or staying late, Brady said he's willing to do what he has to do to be prepared for every game.

"Even though you're not with the first team all the time, you just try to prepare, that's the role of a backup quarterback," Brady said. "You take snaps just to be ready."

And Brady thinks he's ready, no matter his position on the depth chart. ◆

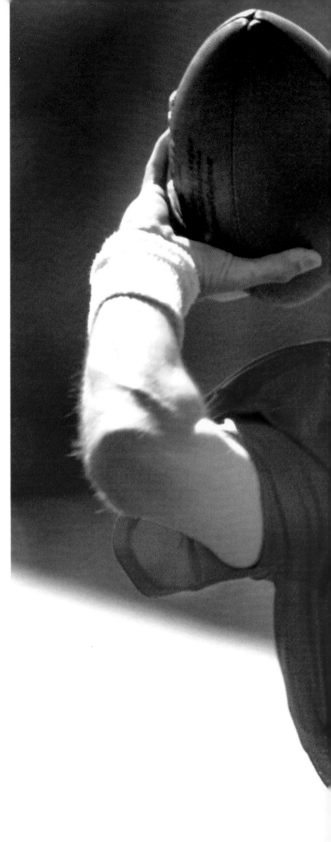

It may look a little awkward, but Brady's passing form works.

2001 SEASON

Game On

by MICHAEL SMITH

September 25, 2001 | He wants this.

That was evident the moment Tom Brady took the podium yesterday for his first press conference as an NFL starting quarterback, if not the night before when he entered the game against the Jets with a little more than two minutes remaining and guided the Patriots to the verge of a tying touchdown.

Yesterday at Foxboro Stadium, Brady — grinning, confident, clearly excited — turned the tables on the media and fired the first question. "Who wants to shoot?" the second-year pro asked, as if to say, "Bring it."

The Indianapolis Colts — next Sunday's opponent — and every other foe promises to bring it as long as Brady, owner of 13 NFL passes and zero starts, fills in for Drew Bledsoe, who yesterday was in stable condition at Massachusetts General Hospital after suffering internal bleeding Sunday night.

That leaves it to Brady to try to right an offense that has managed a combined 20 points in losses to Cincinnati and New York.

Bring it.

"I'm the type of person where, if I ever got that opportunity and didn't play as well as I think I thought I was capable of, I'd be kicking myself until I got another opportunity," said Brady, who at this time last season was the Patriots' fourth QB. "When you do get your opportunities, you have to be ready to take advantage."

Brady, 6 feet 4 inches, 220 pounds, created this opportunity for himself in the offseason and preseason. A sixth-round choice two years ago out of Michigan, he impressed Bill Belichick with the way he commanded respect from fellow rookies, in large part because of the intensity with which he ran the scout-team offense. He arrived in the spring bigger and stronger and had a better training camp than fellow backup QB Damon Huard, whom the Patriots signed to a three-year, $3 million deal in the offseason.

Four good showings in as many exhibi-

Above: San Diego's Raylee Johnson is all over the Patriots QB during an October game in Foxborough.

Right: But Brady still manages to complete 33 of 54 passes (364 yards, 2 TDS) en route to the overtime win.

tion games earned Brady a promotion from No. 3 to No. 2 before the season opener, and his poise in the final moments of Sunday's 10-3 loss reassured Belichick that Brady is right for the job, even though Huard has six years of experience and a 5-1 career record as a starter.

"I thought he did OK with what he had there," Belichick said. "All things considered, I thought in that situation he threw the ball pretty accurately and made good decisions."

Brady entered with 2:16 to go, and led the Patriots on an 11-play, 46-yard drive. He completed 5 of 10 passes on the possession, connecting three times with Troy Brown and once with David Patten for 21 yards. As he has so often in practice, Brady exhibited poise, and he flashed some mobility on a 9-yard scramble.

But the comeback bid fell short, as three consecutive end zone heaves fell incomplete. He didn't provide the Patriots with a victory, but he did provide the offense with a spark, and Belichick thinks it could be a sign of things to come.

"I really don't think that I'm going be standing here week after week talking about all the problems Tom Brady had," Belichick said. "I have confidence in him, I think the team has confidence in him, I think he'll prepare himself and go out there and perform at a good level.

"I'm sure that, like every other young player, there will be something in the game you'd like to be done differently.

But he'll perform overall in the framework of the offense that we've designed for him and he'll make plays that he's capable of making. That's what my expectations are, and Tom will work hard to respond to that opportunity." He shouldn't have to work much harder than he already does. Brady says he always prepares for games as though he'll start, and Belichick has lauded his work ethic.

"I always take the same approach," Brady said. "That I'm going to be in there playing, whether it be a situation like last night, where I'm coming off the bench, or I'm starting the game." Since Brady and Huard are similar in style to Bledsoe, the offense won't have to make as much of an adjustment as it would if, say, a running quarterback like Michael Bishop were playing.

And while the game plan probably will be scaled back a bit for Brady, it won't change drastically, since he and Huard run the same plays in practice as Bledsoe does.

But at 24, Brady isn't, and isn't expected to be, Bledsoe.

"You know there's going to be a drop-off from Drew to Tom," said linebacker Bryan Cox, who experienced similar situations with Dan Marino in Miami and Vinny Testaverde in New York.

"That's not to say that Tom's not capable. I think he's very capable. But it's up to the whole team; it's not just up to Tom Brady to fill this void."

If Brady does as good a job directing the offense as he did of masking any anxiety he may have about his first start, he should do fine.

He was asked whether playing in front of 80,000 college football fans in Ann Arbor, Mich., prepared him for the big stage. "It was 112,000," he said matter-of-factly.

Which explains his answer when asked if he would be nervous. "Not a bit, man," he said. "Not a bit. I prepare as hard as I can every week. I was ready to start last night if they told me to start last night. I'll be just as ready this week." ♦

> "All things considered, I thought in that situation he threw the ball pretty accurately and made good decisions."

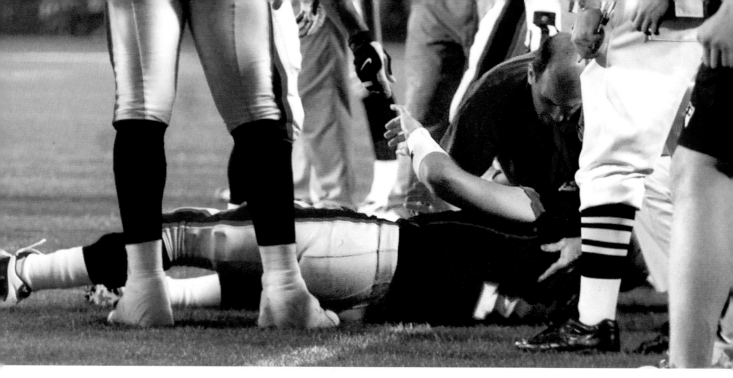

Patriots quarterback Drew Bledsoe is examined by team doctor Bert Zarins after being hit in the fourth quarter of a history-altering September game.

QB Controversy

by DAN SHAUGHNESSY

November 22, 2001 | All he wants to do is play football.

It's what he's always done. He's confident, almost cocky, poised, and dedicated to the craft of playing quarterback. He didn't ask for all this other stuff.

But the other stuff is thrust upon him now. Tom Brady is not just the starting quarterback of the Patriots. He is the Man Who Shot Liberty Valance. He is Jay Leno trying to make us laugh while filling the big shoes of Johnny Carson.

Brady is the Patriots' quarterback and Drew Bledsoe is the $100 million backup. Brady came into this season having thrown three NFL passes, completing one for 6 yards.

Bledsoe came in with a heavy resume that included a Super Bowl, three Pro Bowls, and more passes thrown in eight seasons than any NFL quarterback in history other than Brett Favre.

But Bill Belichick has decided that Brady is The Man. The Patriots are 5-3 under Brady since Bledsoe was hurt in Game 2 against the Jets. Even though Bledsoe says he is healthy and ready to play, Belichick has anointed Brady as the starter for the rest of the season unless "something unforeseen" happens.

It is an awkward situation to say the least. Brady is 24 years old and spent the 2000 season holding a clipboard and learning from Drew in practice and during games. They became friends and Brady has been to the Bledsoe home many times.

Brady is a sixth-round draft pick who makes a paltry (by NFL standards) $298,000. He's been the kid brother to Drew. Now he's got Drew's job. It's a role reversal, like Richie Cunningham suddenly became cooler than the Fonz, George Harrison selling more records than Lennon and McCartney. It's the sophomore younger brother making varsity while the senior older brother is sent to the JV. Awkward. For everyone.

Out of respect to Drew, Brady declined comment Tuesday when the decision came down, but yesterday he spoke with the media and was typically confident, refreshing, and candid.

"There are feelings you fight," he admitted. "One of your teammates and friends isn't as happy as he normally is . . . I don't know if uncomfortable is the word. You want to play and anticipate playing. Someone else not being in the situation they want to be in, it's definitely a difficult situation."

We peppered him with all the standard inquiries — questions that have no good answers. One scribe recalled Brady back in the day saying something to the effect of, "I'm just filling in. It's Drew's job when he's ready to play again." Brady said he couldn't remember making such a remark.

In fact, it doesn't really matter what he said or when he said it. He's been dubbed the starting QB and it's up to Belichick to explain the decision. Brady's job is to beat New Orleans Sunday.

But what about the strain between friends?

"I'm trying to prepare for the game," said Brady. "That's the only strain I have. My goal is to win on Sunday. I'm not trying to beat somebody out. I'm trying to beat the Saints.

"Drew and I talk all the time. I enjoy his friendship and mentorship. I don't see that changing. Obviously, this is a topic of conversation. It almost seems like if you like one person, you have to dislike the other. But that's not the way it is."

Brady sometimes seems too good to be true. He's the unwashed phenom, delivered from Central Casting. He's young, tall, handsome, irreverent, full of hope and promise. He wears his baseball cap backward, like any kid you'd see at the local mall playing video games.

When he explained why it was important to make a decision on one quarterback, Belichick made it sound as if Brady suffered last Sunday because some of his practice time went to Bledsoe. Ever-candid, Brady shot down the notion and said, "No, I was as prepared as I've ever been. I prepare myself the same every week."

Bledsoe may be getting sick of the smiling understudy getting all the practice snaps and newfound glory, but Brady isn't going to say anything to inflame the situation.

"Drew's been more supportive than I could have hoped for," he said. "Our relationship has taken on a different role and I completely understand that. We've always been friends. He's been here nine years and he's done a great job."

At Michigan, Brady went through this same type of situation, but saw it from Bledsoe's side (Brady fought off challenges from Drew Henson). "I know the feeling," said Brady. "He thinks he deserves it and that's where the sympathy comes from."

He went on to say that sympathy was the wrong word. But he wanted us to know that he understands what it's like to be Drew these days.

Brady is good. He was born to be part of a quarterback controversy. He is thus far handling it perfectly. Now we need to see how he does on the field. There was less pressure when he was the understudy, forced to play while Drew recovered. Now he's The Man and everything has changed. ◆

A young QB has high fives for everybody when his team is about to steal an important come-from-behind victory. This Oct. 14 victory over the San Diego Chargers puts Brady on the map.

Family Guy

by BELLA ENGLISH

December 22, 2001 | Everyone knows by now that Patriots quarterback Tom Brady has a good arm and cleft chin. **But did you know that his favorite color is blue? (Like his eyes.)**

That he's left-handed but throws right-handed? (Swings a golf club from the right, a baseball bat from the left.) That onion rings are his favorite food? That he drives a Dodge Ram pickup? (An improvement over the Dodge Dart he bought off his sister when he turned 16.) Also, that he talks nearly every day to his parents in California? (And to his three older sisters, who admit to spoiling him rotten.)

The Patriots' fans have spoiled him, too. Today, he's hotter than a ferry reservation to Martha's Vineyard in August. But New England football — and fans — being as fickle as the local weather, his theme song should be "Will You Still Love Me Tomorrow?" This afternoon he leads the Patriots against the Miami Dolphins in the biggest game of his career so far — if the Patriots win, they take control of their division.

His father, Thomas Edward Brady Sr., is not at all surprised at his son's success. "In many respects, obviously, it's surreal. Twelve weeks ago, no one knew who he was. Now, all of a sudden, he's the feel-good story of the NFL."

Yep, he's the flavor of the season, and it could well be described as an all-American vanilla. "It sounds like an advertisement, but he's every father's dream," says Brady Sr., who describes his son as "my best friend, apart from my wife."

Brady himself says of his family: "It's one of my favorite things to talk about." At 24, he is the youngest of four children of Galynn and Tom Sr. He grew up in San Mateo, Calif., a comfortable suburb south of San Francisco, where his father owns an employee benefits consulting company. For 12 years, he attended Catholic school and served as an altar boy. He played several sports, graduated with a 3.5 grade point average and was drafted out of high school — by the Montreal Expos baseball team. He decided to go to college instead and headed for the University of Michigan, where he graduated with a 3.3 in organizational studies.

"I was a huge baseball player when I was younger," he says during a recent interview in the Patriots' locker room. He's wearing sweats, a Pats tee, and a backwards baseball cap. (Off the premises, he prefers a scally cap.) "After football, baseball was my next favorite sport." Actually, Brady was a relative latecomer to football; his parents wouldn't let him play in the Pop Warner league with his friends because they were afraid of injuring young bones that were still growing.

"Frankly, we didn't really subscribe to football at that age," says Brady Sr. So the boy played baseball, soccer, and basketball, following in the footsteps of his athletic sisters, who all played sports in high school and college. "One year," says his father, "we had 315 games between the four of them, and that didn't include practices." His mother, 57, is a jock, too: Her United States

Blue eyes, cleft chin, backwards baseball cap, boyish grin. What's not to love?

Tennis Association team was the runner-up last year in the national championship.

It wasn't until his freshman year at Junipero Serra High School that Brady picked up a football. He was the backup quarterback who didn't get on the field. (Sound familiar?) But when he was a sophomore, the kid who played in front of him quit, and Brady became the junior varsity starter, moving to varsity the next year. "I spoke to his father at the end of his JV season and told him I thought Tom was definitely a major college prospect as far as his throwing arm went," says his high school coach, Tom MacKenzie.

Everyone thought Brady would go to Cal-Berkeley, which was recruiting him heavily. But when he came back from visiting Michigan, his mind was made up. "It was a soul-searching time for us," says his father. "It was very hard for us to let him go. He's extremely close to us and his sisters."

Why did he do it, then? "Michigan said, 'We have six quarterbacks. You're going to have to compete.' And Tommy said, 'I've got to compete with the best to be the best,'" says his dad.

Brady's parents have flown to every game this season; they'll be in the stands today. To this day, his mother cannot watch her son get sacked. During last week's game against the Buffalo Bills, when he was hit so hard his helmet flew off, his oldest sister, Maureen, left her spot in front of the TV in tears.

"It's not fun watching the games," says his father. "It's exciting, but it's not fun." Last year, Brady's parents came to only a few games, since Brady was the third-string quarterback and left the bench only once.

But that was before star quarterback Drew Bledsoe got injured, before Brady stepped in, started winning games, and was named the new starter. Brady, a second-year player who was a sixth-round draft pick, will earn $298,000 in base salary this year — which is about what Bledsoe makes in a half. Bledsoe and Brady share side-by-side lockers and are friends. Brady refers to Bledsoe as a mentor and has been seen hugging him on the sidelines after a good play. Bledsoe, healthy now but on the bench, has praised Brady's playing but has grown tired of all the questions about the awkward situation. "Can we give it a rest?" he asked a reporter recently.

Tom Brady Sr. doesn't shy away from the subject. "Drew has been so good for New England for so long that what has occurred to Tommy this year is almost as if the good Lord said, 'Tommy, we're going to bless you this year and give you the opportunity.' It was something so far out of anyone's consciousness until Drew got hurt. When he was hurt, Tommy was hurt for him. On the other hand, having the opportunity to play is what he has worked so darn many hours to do. It's the pain of the game."

DESIRE TO WIN

The young Brady has been in this fight before. At Michigan, he was the understudy quarterback behind Brian Griese, son of football legend Bob Griese. When Griese graduated, Brady got the starting spot, only to nearly lose it his senior year — when he was team captain — to a freshman. Head football coach Lloyd Carr remembers alternating the two players to see who would get the nod.

"Tom handled it with class. He'd always had the starting job, and he was in an extremely competitive battle, but in the end, he prevailed. He couldn't be dislodged." Carr says he isn't surprised at Brady's success this season. "In my experience, he's one of the real special people, one of the great competitors... He's tough; he's smart; he has great desire and determination to improve; he has tremendous leadership skills.

"It's hard to believe," he continues, "that a guy could be as well mannered and decent, and on that football field, he'll cut you up." Indeed, it is said that the laid-back Brady turns super-intense in a huddle, exhorting his teammates, in colorful language, to destroy the opponent.

"Without a doubt, he's a good leader. He's always focused. He's always positive."
—former Pats receiver David Patten

This competitor lives for high-pressure situations, including fourth down and inches with the game on the line. His faithfully viewing family members, on the other hand, might prefer a little less drama. "It's not fun watching the games," says Tom Brady Sr. "It's exciting, but it's not fun."

"Without a doubt, he's a good leader," says Patriots wide receiver David Patten. "He's always focused. He's always positive. He always has a smile on his face, even on the rough days." As for the Bledsoe-Brady face-off, he says: "We all know Drew wants his job back, but it's Tom's now. They're both handling it well. They're always cracking jokes."

Ian Gold, who played with Brady at Michigan and is now a linebacker for the Denver Broncos, says he, for one, is surprised at Brady's newfound success. "I knew he'd be a successful quarterback, but as far as how soon, that's really surprising. That he'd be replacing Drew Bledsoe... I wouldn't have taken that bet in a million years."

Still, he's a Brady fan. "He's not the greatest athlete in the world, but he uses his brain. He's got a great arm, but he's not the fastest guy. He'd take his big hits left and right. He'd get hammered, but he'd get up with so much intensity, you could just see the fire in his eyes. Guys like playing with him. I'd go to war with Tom any day."

Yes, the 6-foot-4, 220-pound Brady has taken plenty of hits. But ask him about his worst injury, and he'll mention the emergency appendectomy when he was a junior in college.

It's when he talks about his family that his face lights up. It's as if they are, indeed, the happily-ever-after Brady Bunch. "I've got three older sisters," he says, "and I get spoiled by all of them, and my parents." Maureen is 28, Julie 27, and Nancy 25. All live within 30 miles of their parents in California.

On July 1, Brady flew home to surprise his family. That night, Maureen delivered a baby girl, two weeks early. "Maya's pictures are all over my house," says Brady. "That baby's lucky to come into our family, because there's a lot

> "He's a good man. He loves kids. He loves his family. ... Growing up with three sisters he really knows how to treat women."

of love. "I think I just always followed the example they set for me, to be respectful of everybody everyday, to always appreciate where you've been. My dad always says, 'To whom much is given, much is expected.'"

He's having fun this year, but he's beginning to feel the press of being in the spotlight. "I hardly have any free time," he says. "I have a hard time saying no to people, and I have to learn how to do that more often." Remembering the adolescent thrill of getting Hall of Fame quarterback Joe Montana's autograph, he signs autograph after autograph. "It's a lot different from last year." His grin accentuates the dimple in his square chin.

He complains about "getting worn thin" and "being distracted" by the new demands on his time. "We have one day off a week. Well, really, quarterbacks have half a day off. I use it to pay bills, do the laundry, and clean the house." The former high school baseball catcher sometimes stops by local batting cages, loves to play golf, and hangs out at a popular jock watering hole in Boston.

"I like to hang with those guys. We can all relate," he says. On a recent night, he chatted with Celtics star Antoine Walker. "He always comes in with a buddy, and he's always wearing a baseball cap," said Heather Michalowski, the bar's spokeswoman. "He brings in his own bottled water. He's very well mannered and polite."

"I've always said that whatever girl gets him is going to be the luckiest one in the world," says big sister Maureen. "He's a good man. He loves kids. He loves his family. I guess growing up with three sisters he really knows how to treat women and he understands them. He's a little sweetheart. He's tough on the field, but off the field, with us girls, he's pretty sentimental."

Tom Brady is winning now, but how does he handle losing? "I don't lose very much. You don't play to lose," he says. It's not brag; it's fact. Those who know him say he's not arrogant but self-confident. "He struggled with being patient with himself," says MacKenzie, his high school coach. "He's a perfectionist."

Says former teammate Gold: "Most quarterbacks tend to get a big head. He never did. He stayed humble."

Mark Farinella, who has covered the Patriots for the Attleboro Sun Chronicle for 25 years, finds his attitude refreshing. "Tom Brady came in and right off the bat, he had that childlike enthusiasm. His attitude is, he's going to enjoy every minute of this. Most guys try to internalize it. Brady exudes it."

This week, it was announced that Brady won the New England Patriots 12th Player Award, presented annually to the player who performs above fan expectations. It's determined by fan voting.

If the Patriots win today, it will indeed be a very Brady Christmas for him and his family. And if they lose, well, at least his family — if not the fans — will still adore him. ◆

From the moment he stepped into Bledsoe's shoes, there's been a very Brady quality to football in New England.

Fantastic finish

by BOB FEDAS

February 2, 2002 | Many "experts" predicted that 2001 would produce the Patriots' third consecutive last-place finish in the AFC East. But after a shaky start, Bill Belichick & Co. ended the regular season with a six-game winning streak to set their march to the Super Bowl in motion.

GAME 1   9-9-01
CINCINNATI 23 | NE 17   AWAY

It was a day of missed opportunities for the Patriots — mostly missing opportunities to tackle Bengals running back Corey Dillon, who rushed for 104 yards and a touchdown on 24 carries. Big plays also hurt New England, and a late-game effort unraveled when Drew Bledsoe got hit with multiple sacks. **Record: 0-1.**

GAME 2   9-23-01
NY JETS 10 | NE 3   HOME

This was the game that changed the Patriots' season. At 4:48 of the fourth quarter, Bledsoe, hoping to run for a first down, received a brutal hit from Jets linebacker Mo Lewis. The veteran returned for one series but then gave way — it would later be determined he'd suffered a life-threatening chest injury — to Tom Brady.

The second-year quarterback from Michigan guided the Patriots to a pair of first downs in their search for the tying score, but two passes into the end zone at the end of the game fell incomplete. Curtis Martin ran for 106 yards and a touchdown on 24 carries, helping the Jets give Herman Edwards his first career coaching victory. **Record: 0-2.**

GAME 3   9-30-01
NE 44 | INDIANAPOLIS 13   HOME

With Bledsoe out nursing a sheared blood vessel, Brady capably commanded the Patriots' offense as his teammates played easily their best game of the young season. New England rushed for 177 yards (92 and two touchdowns by Antowain Smith) and got interception returns for touchdowns from Otis Smith (78 yards) and Ty Law (23 yards). Once again, Belichick and his defensive staff frustrated Colts quarterback Peyton Manning, who fell to 0-4 at Foxboro Stadium. **Record: 1-2.**

GAME 4 — 10-7-01

MIAMI 30 | NE 10   **AWAY**

So much for the step forward. This week, Dolphins running back Lamar Smith nearly outgained the Patriots on his own, rushing for 144 yards and a score as the swarming Miami defense limited New England to 149 total yards. Brady, who had been asked to do little against the Colts, could do even less against the Dolphins as he completed 12 of 24 attempts for 86 yards. **Record: 1-3.**

GAME 5 — 10-14-01

NE 29 | SAN DIEGO 26 | OT HOME

The game that truly put Brady on the map. The young quarterback (33 of 54, 364 yards, 2 TDs) led the Patriots to come from behind and force overtime. In the extra session, after the Chargers went three-and-out, Brady guided his team from their 23 into San Diego territory, getting Adam Vinatieri in position for his winning 44-yarder. **Record: 2-3.**

GAME 6 — 10-21-01

NE 38 | INDIANAPOLIS 17 AWAY

Patriots receiver David Patten assumed a starring role, becoming the first player since Walter Payton to run, catch, and pass for TDs in the same game. Brady picked up where he left off against the Chargers, completing 16 of 20 throws for 202 yards and three scores. Manning was not his usual ineffective self against the Patriots, throwing for 335 yards, but he was pressured relentlessly, and the Colts' defense couldn't contain the Patriots, who went deep into the offensive playbook, scoring on a 29-yard Patten reverse and a 60-yard pass from Patten to Troy Brown. **Record: 3-3.**

Above: Injured veteran signal caller Bledsoe is around on the sidelines to offer advice and encouragement.

Above right: But Brady's the one who takes the hit when the Rams beat the Patriots in Game 10.

GAME 8   11-4-01

NE 24 | ATLANTA 10   **AWAY**

Brady displayed the kind of short-term memory that serves quarterbacks well as he rebounded by hitting on 21 of 31 passes for 250 yards and three scores, while Smith rushed for 117 yards. But if Brady was the No. 1 star, the Patriots' defense was 1A. It registered nine sacks and limited the Falcons to 104 passing yards. **Record: 4-4.**

GAME 9   11-11-01

NE 21 | BUFFALO 11   **HOME**

The Bills proved to be tougher opponents than their 1-6 record would suggest. The outcome wasn't decided until Smith (20 carries, 100 yards) sealed his former team's fate with a 42-yard touchdown run with 1:52 remaining. The Patriots were above .500 for the first time since December 1999. **Record: 5-4.**

GAME 7   10-28-01

DENVER 31 | NE 20   **AWAY**

New England led, 20-10, early in the third quarter but then began to unravel, unable to stop Brian Griese & Co., then coughing up the ball on offense. Brady, who had thrown an NFL-record 162 straight passes without an interception to start his career, was picked off four times in the fourth quarter as the Broncos rattled off 21 unanswered points for the victory. **Record: 3-4.**

GAME 10   11-18-01

ST. LOUIS 24 | NE 17   **HOME**

Rams quarterback Kurt Warner wowed a Sunday night national television audience by throwing for 401 yards and three touchdowns. He also threw two interceptions (one of which was returned 52 yards for a TD by Terrell Buckley) and fumbled once, but still came out ahead. **Record: 5-5.**

49

GAME 11   11-25-01

NE 34 | NEW ORLEANS 17   **HOME**

Shortly after the loss to the Rams, Belich-ick said he would be sticking with Brady as his quarterback even though Bledsoe had been cleared to play by doctors. The coach was vindicated as Brady threw for 258 yards and a career-high four touch-downs in a dominant effort. Smith, who rushed for 111 yards on 24 carries, was on the receiving end of one of Brady's TD throws, taking a screen pass 41 yards to pay dirt. Brady also hit Brown, Charles Johnson, and Marc Edwards for scores as the Patriots racked up 432 total yards, making what had been billed as a strong Saints defense look porous. **Record: 6-5.**

GAME 12   12-2-01

NE 17 | NY JETS 16   **AWAY**

Trailing 13-0, the Patriots must have paid close attention to Belichick's "our season is on the line" speech at halftime. After the break, the Patriots pulled out all the stops, even calling on little-known receiver Fred Coleman, who caught a slant pass from Brady and scurried 46 yards, setting up Smith's 4-yard run that brought the Patriots to 13-7. Vinatieri put the Patriots in front with a 28-yard field goal with 6:29 remain-ing, and then with the Jets driving toward the winning score, Buckley intercepted Vin-ny Testaverde. Brady's 2-yard run on third and 2 iced it, setting off an avalanche of emotion from Belichick, who ran around the field hugging his players. **Record: 7-5.**

Brady makes the most of a snow day — the Jan. 19 divisional playoff, one of the greatest wins in Patriots history.

GAME 13   12-9-01

NE 27 | CLEVELAND 16   **HOME**

Brown submitted his usual stellar all-around performance, catching seven passes for 89 yards and returning a punt 85 yards to put the Patriots ahead to stay. **Record: 8-5.**

GAME 14   12-16-01

NE 12 | BUFFALO 9 | OT   **AWAY**

If it's ever good for a player to be uncon-scious, such was the case for the Patriots in overtime. After catching a 13-yard pass from Brady on the Patriots' first posses-sion in the extra session, Patten lost con-trol of the ball at the Bills' 41-yard line. The Bills recovered, but when the play was reviewed, it was determined that Patten, during the seconds he was unconscious from Keion Carpenter's hit, was touch-ing out of bounds (with his head) and the ball (with his calf), meaning the Patriots retained possession. They got Vinatieri into position and he booted the winning 23-yarder. **Record: 9-5.**

GAME 15   12-22-01

NE 20 | MIAMI 13   HOME

In the final regular-season game at Foxboro Stadium, the Patriots went out on top, overtaking the Dolphins for first place in the AFC East. Smith ran for a career-high 156 yards and a TD. **Record: 10-5.**

GAME 16   1-6-02

NE 38 | CAROLINA 6   AWAY

The Patriots shook off what little rust there was after their bye week and crushed the Panthers, who set an NFL record with their 15th straight loss. With some help, New England also earned a first-round bye in the playoffs. Brown had a 68-yard touchdown punt return, and six catches giving him a team-record 101 for the season. The Patriots forced six turnovers. **Record: 11-5.**

DIVISIONAL PLAYOFF   1-19-02

NE 16 | OAKLAND 13 | OT | HOME

The final game at Foxboro Stadium turned out to be one of its most memorable because of (A) a driving snowstorm, (B) the stakes, (C) the Patriots' heroics, and (D) referee Walt Coleman.

The Raiders thought they had snuffed out the Patriot's last flicker of hope when, with 1:50 remaining, cornerback Charles Woodson hit Brady, forcing the ball loose, and linebacker Greg Biekert pounced on it. But when Coleman went under the hood to check out the replay, he determined that

Brady, after bringing his arm forward, had not tucked the ball against his body, meaning it was an incomplete forward pass. New England retained possession and moments later Vinatieri connected on a 45-yard low-liner of a field goal to send the game into overtime.

After winning the toss to start the extra period, the Patriots drove 61 yards before Vinatieri came on to hammer the winning 23-yarder. **Record: 12-5.**

AFC CHAMPIONSHIP   1-27-02

NE 24 | PITTSBURGH 17 | AWAY

Special teams left no doubt that the Patriots are indeed a special team. Sparked by Brown's 55-yard punt return for the game's first score and Antwan Harris's 49-yard runback of a blocked punt, the Patriots advanced to their third Super Bowl.

Brady (ankle) was knocked from the game in the second quarter by a low hit from Pittsburgh safety Lee Flowers, bringing on Bledsoe for the first time since Week 2. All Bledsoe did was connect on three straight passes (all to Patten), the final one into the corner of the end zone for an 11-yard touchdown and a 14-3 halftime edge.

The lead increased to 21-3 when Brandon Mitchell broke through the Pittsburgh line and blocked Kris Brown's field goal attempt. The ball was picked up by Troy Brown, who lateraled to Harris, who raced to the end zone. Kordell Stewart led the Steelers on a pair of third-quarter touchdown drives, bringing them within 21-17, but Vinatieri upped the Patriots' lead with a 44-yard field goal, and late interceptions ensured the Patriots another trip to New Orleans. **Record: 13-5.**

Above: Even Colts defender Chukie Nwokorie can't stop the Patriots from rolling to a 44-13 rout in September.

Left: But Denver does the job in October, when Brady and company fall to the Broncos, 31-20.

SUPER BOWL XXXVI

Poised

by KEVIN PAUL DUPONT

February 3, 2002 | The Louisiana lawn is a lot like New Orleans, a facade; actually a faux fauna that probably favors the Rams tonight in their Super Bowl showdown with the Patriots.

At the start of the season, few people believed this unheralded and inexperienced young quarterback could bring his team anywhere near a Super Bowl, never mind actually win one.

The Rams are built for speed, with speed, and the green broadloom turf inside the Superdome figures to play right into the hands and legs of their devilishly fast receivers and the laser-accurate throwing arm of Kurt Warner. Little did New England quarterback Tom Brady figure, back when he penned his high school farewell, that the words below his picture would prove to be so prophetic, even if a slightly off botanical metaphor.

> "If you want to play with the big boys... you gotta learn to play in the tall grass."

"If you want to play with the big boys," Brady scrawled below his likeness in the Junipero Serra High yearbook, "you gotta learn to play in the tall grass."

Barely known in the NFL when the season began, truly a September footnote even to serious Foxboroughologists, the 24-year-old Brady now leads the Patriots into Super Bowl XXXVI. The San Mateo, Calif., kid with the broad smile, the square cleft chin, and a natural well of enthusiasm the envy of Poland Springs gets to wing it with Warner in the shortest but most significant grass of all.

Not long ago he was just another of Michigan's many fine quarterbacks, so much a part of the Ann Arbor woodwork that he was still around at pick No. 199 when it came time for the Patriots to select in the sixth round of the 2000 draft. Skinny, thin-necked, wiry Tommy Brady, the youngest of Tom and Galynn's four kids, who didn't pick up a football until his freshman year in high school because his parents thought it might be too rough a game for their only son. Now he's here, front and under center, with a chance by late tonight to be telling the world that, yeah, aw shucks, he'll go to Disney World, and that he couldn'tuh done it without Drew Bledsoe, loves the Bay State like it was the Bay Area, figures Charlie Weis oughta be callin' bigger plays in the Pentagon,

will buy each of his offensive linemen a time-share (say, Week 7 or 8, to avoid a possible perennial conflict with Week 4 or 5), and that Bill Belichick, well, is just so cool that there are times he looks at the lovable lug and sees a guy under those layers of coaching garb that was just born, just born to be a surfin' dude.

Not that Brady even hinted at any of that last week (apologies, offensive linemen) because, in true Brady fashion, the former altar boy remained nothing but humble and genuine and engaging in all his dealings with the media. He showed up here with a sore ankle, pulled like taffy by the Steelers in last Sunday's AFC championship game, and by Wednesday night was pronounced fit and able to make his 17th straight start for the Patriots.

What, you expected different? Nossir. Same ol', same ol'. Brady is back, armor spit-shined. All that remains to be seen is how the next chapter of the fairy tale will read.

"You know, everybody talks about Brett this, Brett that," said ESPN analyst Joe Theismann, the former NFL quarterback, noting the many talents of Packers quarterback Brett Favre. "Let me tell you, when Tom Brady wants to step back and cut it loose, I'll match his arm with anybody in this league — but the thing is, he's accurate. When he sets to fire, he can fire."

There is no test in the developmental process quite like a Super Bowl. Truly a rookie, after only one three-pass relief appearance last season, Brady may look back years from now at this game as the final exam that convinced one and all, perhaps even himself, that he'd arrived in the league. A win would guarantee it.

The impact of a New England loss? Though devastating to everyone in Patriots Nation, it most likely would be viewed as just the final dance in what has been Brady's four-month, mesmerizing coming-out party. Rarely in recent memory has New England witnessed so enthralling a debut. The most memorable: Ted Williams. Bobby Orr. Larry Bird. Tony

Joe Theismann says of Brady's accurate arm: "When he sets to fire, he can fire."

Conigliaro. Fred Lynn.

"Oh," said Theismann, "he's going to be fun to watch grow into this league."

If not for Bledsoe's sheared blood vessel in Week 2, of course, all most of the world would know of Brady today probably would be his status as the smiling, eager-to-learn kid on the sideline who went 20-5 in his two years of starts in Michigan. World of potential, that 6-foot-4-inch Brady kid, but just a good-natured backup bauble to hold a clipboard and wear headphones on game day.

Truth is, no one knew what they had in Brady, not even the Patriots, which in part makes the story all the more engaging, especially when compared to a similar story in St. Louis. Until St. Louis homeboy

QB Trent Green ripped up a knee in the '99 exhibition season, all that the world knew of Kurt Warner was a quirky pedigree that included Division 1-AA's Northern Iowa, the Iowa Barnstormers of the Arena League, and the Amsterdam Admirals of NFL Europe.

Brady is a stretch? Then Warner was, and is, a tale scripted for instant rejection by the Grade "B" Movie Board of Cinematic Arts. What next, a multi-film series in wunderkind wizards?

"There are certain similarities," agreed Brady, noting the comparison to 30-year-old Warner. "But then other parts are not similar — the opportunity presented for him, he went in and did really well and took over. I think that is quite a bit different than what we have here. Drew was injured, and I came in, played 15 games, and I think there is still lot to be decided."

Ever Brady. Diplomatic from the tip of the Red Sox cap he wore everywhere in New Orleans, down to the tip of his sneakers.

"I think maybe if you look back in a couple of years," he added, clearly uncomfortable when projecting his future vis a vis Bledsoe, "there probably will be more similarities, or less similarities, but at this point, that is our situation."

All of it sheds slight on the mystery/inexact science of scouting. Warner was never drafted. Brady was the seventh quarterback taken in what was considered a weak class for signal-callers. Now they're matching wits in the world's biggest football game.

What, precisely, do they do at those NFL combines? Today we will watch two guys considered to be the CEOs of their craft, who, in the eyes of the combine, didn't qualify for the lunchroom, never mind the boardroom.

"With the combine and scouts, it's like they put all their emphasis into certain people — you know, guys who are supposed to be The Guys — and a lot of guys get overlooked," said Rams guard Kaulana Noa, the 104th pick in the 2000 draft. "They don't measure the heart of somebody, or the will to work, and a lot of that gets unnoticed, because maybe they are not physically as tall or as strong. But a lot of guys still know how to play the game."

The factors are opportunity and projection. Scouts and personnel directors first must factor the player's collegiate track record, within the framework of the college he has played for, and estimate how the player will develop if given a chance to play. "I think what it says is that it just makes this game great, the NFL, that those things can happen in the league," said Rams coach Mike Martz. "It's no reflection that someone isn't doing their job or doesn't know what they are doing — it is just, well, that's life."

Gil Brandt, former vice president for personnel of the Dallas Cowboys, figures the lesson in it all is that scouts have to be diligent about rating a quarterback prospect's intelligence and work ethic. "When you listen to Brady, and he talks about how 80 percent of the plays are different from week to week — and the guy understands the offense — well, obviously he is smart," said Brandt.

"But there are a lot of smart guys who don't take time to work, and work ethic is a big, big factor. I think for most quarterbacks it comes down to accuracy, mental toughness, and intelligence.

There are some guys, hey, they don't have the greatest ability but they get the job done. Guys like Billy Kilmer and that, they didn't have the greatest ability. Bobby Lane is another. My hat goes off to Brady, and my hat goes off to Belichick to stick with him."

READY AND WILLING

For 6-8 weeks, Belichick had little choice but to go with the former Montreal catching prospect (18th-round pick in 1995). Based on preseason performance, the coaching staff

---

Nothing fancy. Nothing flashy. Just shoot straight and get the job done.

leapfrogged Brady ahead of ex-Miami quarterback Damon Huard on the depth chart. The latter, once Dan Marino's understudy, moved to third-wheel status, backing the $298,000-per-year Brady.

"Controversial," is what offensive coordinator Charlie Weis still labels the decision. "We brought in Damon Huard to be backup — and by the way, Huard is the one quarterback in the world to beat Kurt Warner twice, as he [recently] let me know. We brought in Huard, who had a 5-1 record as a starter, did a good job with Marino down in Miami, and in training camp Damon wasn't a bust, he was pretty good.

"But we saw something in training camp that made us decide to make Tom No. 2. It's all the things you've seen when he plays — that same special type of thing. We wanted it that if the guy went in, he would have a clue what to do, know how to manage a team. And you have to have the players believe in a quarterback, believe they can win when he is in."

It is that readiness factor that provided Brady with the initial burst of success, magic, charisma. Working with what Weis acknowledges was a trimmed game plan, a schematic that initially featured variety if not volume, Brady had the Patriots marching off the hop with short passes over the top, screens, the occasional long ball. What Brady didn't initiate with his arm, often hooking up with Troy Brown, Antowain Smith made happen with his legs. Arm firing. Wheels whirring.

"From the time I got here," said Brady, "I've just been preparing myself for the opportunity to play. You go through times in college, even those first three years [at Michigan] that I wasn't playing, hey, I was ready to play even if the coach didn't put me in — so when he put me in my fourth year, I was ready to go. The same thing happened here. I prepared myself, hard as I could, mentally and physically, watching and learning from these others guys who have done it. And we've gone out this year and played pretty well."

So well, in fact, that Brady will head to the Pro Bowl when his day is done here. Then there will be the weeks ahead, maybe months, that will determine his future in Foxborough. There is a chance that he will be dealt (what chance, really, if he wins today?) and that Bledsoe will be revived as the franchise QB next season. But it's far more likely that Brady remains in place, the story to play out in years to come, and a new home is found for the veteran warrior.

"He got stronger, and his work ethic has really allowed him to have the year he has had this year," said the diplomatic Bledsoe, remaining unflinching in his public support of Brady, who was a high school sophomore when Bledsoe first came to the Patriots. "It is not an accident that he has come in and played very, very well. He has worked at it, and honestly earned everything he has done this year. As hard as it was to stand there and watch someone else on the field, it also was very gratifying to see one of the truly good guys be rewarded for hard work and dedication he has shown."

A season is about to end, and now the future is ours to see. The ball goes to Brady, the smiling, blue-eyed slinger who grew up dreaming of one day playing in the biggest game of all.

"Let me look at him on film," said Theismann, another to reflect on how talent can sometimes be initially overlooked. "Tell me what his teammates think of him, what his coaches think of him.

Coaches can have a selfish reason for liking guys, or not liking guys. Take Joe Montana. [Former Notre Dame coach] Dan Devine hated him. Now there's a classic example of a guy — a third-round pick, Joe Montana. Yeah, right.

Came out of Notre Dame, didn't play, but they kept sticking him in games that they were losing like, 35-7, and he would end up winning it, 37-35, you know? There is something a little special about a guy like that."

In the whisper of the tall grass, it sounds vaguely familiar. ◆

SWEET YOUTH	At 24, Tom Brady is the youngest quarterback to win a Super Bowl. The five youngest:				
PLAYER	TEAM	YEAR	OPPONENT	SCORE	AGE
Tom Brady	Patriots	2002	Rams	20-17	24
Joe Montana	49ers	1982	Bengals	26-21	25
Joe Namath	Jets	1969	Colts	16-7	25
Troy Aikman	Cowboys	1993	Bills	52-17	26
Jim McMahon	Bears	1986	Patriots	46-10	26

For Real

by BOB RYAN

February 4, 2002 | They say it takes how long to make someone into an effective quarterback in this league?

There no longer can be rules or maxims involving quarterbacks. Tom Brady has shattered all the myths. Henceforth, if you can play, you can play.

There might be other Bradys out there, other second-year players who completed one pass in three attempts as a rookie, who get their chance when the nine-year veteran gets hurt, and who then conclude a 13-3 regular season and playoff combined run by directing their teams downfield in the final 1 minute 21 seconds of the Super Bowl to put them in position for the winning field goal. But don't bet Junior's school lunch money on it.

Brady may be the exception that proves the rule. Brady may be the NFL's single most inexplicable personnel phenomenon, a sixth-round pick who spends the season in extended OJT and winds up as the MVP in the Super Bowl.

When Brady took control of the huddle with that 1:21 left, no timeouts remaining, the ball on the Patriots 17-yard line, and the score tied at 17 after the Patriots had once led by a 17-3 score, his teammates did not see a kid quarterback. They saw a leader.

"You can't say enough about that kid," marveled wide receiver David Patten. "He has a tremendous amount of confidence,

> "That minute-and-30-second drive has got to be one of the biggest drives in Super Bowl history."

and it rubs off on everyone else. You look in his eyes and say, 'Hey, we've got to go down and win it for this kid.'"

"What can I say about Tom Brady?" added linebacker Tedy Bruschi. "That minute-and-30-second drive has got to be one of the biggest drives in Super Bowl history."

"Brady brings a lot of confidence to the team in that huddle," said guard Joe Andruzzi.

Brady's modest final numbers show you what you can do with numbers when the only real issue is what's on the scoreboard. He was 16 for 27 for 145 yards and one touchdown. But in what you would have to agree was a reasonably important game, he threw no interceptions and did nothing stupid. "Tom did a super job of managing the game," lauded coach Bill Belichick.

Brady was only overtly great when he had to be. On that final drive, during which he moved the team from its 17 to the Rams 30 in seven plays before spiking the ball to stop the clock at :07, he completed 5 of 6 passes, the sixth being a simple throwaway. The whole performance was eerily similar to his work in the Snow Bowl two weeks ago, when he likewise saved his best for last.

"He did what his team needed him to do," said Rams quarterback Kurt Warner. "He made the plays on the last drive that got

them the win. He's done that all year. My hat's off to him."

Brady was so fazed by his first Super Bowl that he took a nap upon arrival. "I fell asleep," he reported, "and when I woke up I said to myself I didn't think I'd feel this good. I convinced myself that it was just a game, just another game."

In some ways, it was. Brady mostly threw the short- and medium-route passes that are his trademark. He had enough of a running game to keep the Rams honest. The defense made huge plays. And when Brady had to be more than just competent, when he needed to be special, he entered another realm and made the plays that had to be made.

I am of the firm belief that in the matter of Truth vs. Fiction, especially when it involves your 2001-02 Patriots, it is always wise to take Truth, plus the points.

Like, did Drew Bledsoe, the Big Brother/Mentor/Rival, really instruct Brady just before that final drive to "Go out there and sling it?" Well, yes, he did. And did Brady, needing something more than a dink or dunk job, really hit - guess who? - Troy Brown for 23 yards on second and 10 at the Patriots 41? Of course.

"That was the big play," Brady said. "It's called '64 Max All-End,' and the Max stands for, as my coach says, 'We need the maximum time for me to throw.'"

The throw was around neck high, but Brown, a.k.a. Mr. Reliable, snatched it out of the air and ran out of bounds. "The way the Rams play, they really read the quarterback's eyes. I was looking hard to the right, and Troy slipped behind them. They lost sight of him. I hit him, and he did the rest."

> "I convinced myself that it was just a game, just another game."

That put the ball on the Rams 36. Brady completed one more, to Jermaine Wiggins for 6 yards, spiked the ball, and turned the proceedings over to Adam Vinatieri, who never had missed an indoor field goal attempt - and still hasn't.

This Brady is a kid whose only realistic goal when the season started was "to become a far better player by the time it was over."

The only way he was going to get Bledsoe's job was if Bledsoe got hurt. As for the Super Bowl, please. The Super Bowl. Tom Brady just won the Super Bowl. How bizarre is that?

"I ran into Dan Marino down here," Brady said. "I've never met him before. I know he was in his second year when he went to the Super Bowl, and I asked him what he was thinking about the day after. He said, 'Tommy, I was wishing I could play it over again, because you never know when you'll get back.' It's all about seizing your opportunities."

There are few things in life more disastrous than to receive your big break and not be prepared to make the most of it. When Bledsoe went down, Brady stepped in with aplomb. The other 10 men in the huddle knew he was prepared. He proved himself to be an astonishingly quick learner. He proved himself to be a winner.

Week after week after week other teams in the NFL learned to respect Tom Brady. Now, in the biggest showcase American sport has to offer, Brady has demonstrated to a fascinated American public that he is a special athlete, that he is a certified champion.

The story line is utterly fictional, but Tom Brady is completely real. He is the Truth who has obliterated all the Fiction. ♦

Can you believe it? The winners' platform in New Orleans belongs to Super Bowl MVP Tom Brady and his world champion New England Patriots.

Mr. Clutch

by DAN SHAUGHNESSY

February 5, 2002 | He was on the cover of a Wheaties box before the Patriots' Super Bowl victory was an hour old. He's already emerged as every mother's favorite would-be son-in-law. The man who never throws the bomb now is the bomb.

Above: Being a Super Bowl hero means signing a lot of autographs.

Left: And it can also mean a visit to Boston's hallowed Fenway Park, where you and your teammates (Lawyer Milloy on the left, Tedy Bruschi on the right) help kick off the season for another local team that drives fans crazy.

In Boston professional sports, there never has been anything like The Tom Brady Story. We've had our share of Hall of Famers, franchise players, and unwashed phenoms, but Brady takes the cake. He also takes the Cadillac Escalade (Super Bowl MVP car), the trip to the Pro Bowl, and he'll probably take your kid sister to the prom if you ask him nicely.

What's left? People magazine's Sexiest Man Alive? A stint with the Chicago White Sox? Lighting the Olympic torch in Salt Lake City? The ceremonial first pitch for the Red Sox home opener?

This debate raged in the Big Easy last week when reporters got a good, long look at Brady in daily press conferences... Damon or DiCaprio? By the end of Super Bowl XXXVI, the question was... Marino or Montana?

We've been blessed with greater talents. Certainly no one would equate Brady's skills with those of Ted Williams, Bill Russell, Bobby Orr, or Larry Bird. Fred Lynn had an equally impressive rookie year (and never mind the technicality, this was Brady's rookie year). But those stars came with impressive resumes and accompanying expectations. Brady came needing ID to get into the stadium.

That's what's so amazing. A year ago, Brady was on the roster, but even Patriot fans who were dissatisfied with Drew Bledsoe spent their time talking about Michael Bishop. Brady was a sixth-round draft pick.

Old No. 199. He was a kid who played in one game in 2000-01, throwing three passes against the Detroit Lions, completing one.

And now Brady is the It Guy. In one magical season, he did something Teddy Ballgame and Ray Bourque never did in our town: He won a championship. Helped by a clever, low-risk offensive game plan, Brady rarely makes mistakes that cost games.

You watch him and you listen and it's hard to tell if he understands how great and unbelievable this is. It's as if he expected nothing less... you get a chance to play, you win the Super Bowl. Simple.

Princes of Main Street, Kings of New England, the World Champion Patriots will be feted today in Boston's first championship celebration in 16 years. Brady no doubt will say a few words and they'll be the right words.

He knows nothing of curses and the sky-is-falling mentality that pollutes our sports landscape. He dares to wear a Red Sox cap, sometimes backward. He's quick to talk about his parents and his sisters. He's respectful of his teammates.

And he's clutch. Like Montana. Already.

Remember the blizzard playoff game against the Raiders? Brady completed 32 of 52 passes in those impossible conditions. At one point, he connected on nine straight.

He's also lucky. The whole world knows he fumbled that ball against Oakland, but he was saved by a technicality and the luck of the clock (the Patriots had used up their challenges and the play was reviewed only because less than two minutes remained).

Sunday night in New Orleans, Brady's numbers were quite ordinary and you could have voted for Ty Law or Adam Vinatieri as MVP, but Brady's the one who moved the Patriots 53 yards in the final 1:21 without the benefit of any time outs (while John Madden was saying he should take a knee and go for overtime). Brady completed five passes in the winning drive. Then he hugged Drew Bledsoe.

Then he thanked his parents. Then he signed the Wheaties box for Troy Brown, saying, "Put 53 guys on this box." Then he did a million television interviews.

He held up the Lombardi Trophy and said, "There's a lot of fingerprints on this."

Then he told us he fell asleep before the game. He was napping when Sir Paul McCartney (who recorded an album entitled "Ram," by the way) was singing "Freedom."

Brady is good. He is confident. He gets it. He has been sent from Central Casting. Joe Hardy in shoulder pads. He is too good to be true.

He was a delight in the tedious media sessions in New Orleans. When two reporters asked a question at the same time, he motioned toward the one who looked like Miss Brazil, smiled, and said, "I'd rather answer her question." Later, when a 10-year-old boy asked about the Ram defense, Brady said, "Way to stand up there and ask your question, little man."

Now what? What can you do for an encore when you are 24 years old and you have already been MVP of the Super Bowl?

"I've got to prove it for a lot of years," Brady said. "I've got a long ways to go. I think there's a lot of football left." ♦

> ## What can you do for an encore when you are 24 years old and you have already been MVP of the Super Bowl?

Earned

by PETER MAY

February 5, 2002 | Bill Belichick likes to reward his players for diligent offseason work, and last spring, Tom Brady was deemed to be the most improved player at his position. His prize — a preferred parking spot at training camp.

"It may not seem like much, but [the players] like to park 2 inches closer to the meeting rooms and dorms than anybody else," the New England Patriots coach said yesterday, less than 12 hours removed from the team's improbable 20-17 victory over the Rams in Super Bowl XXXVI. "Tom had this kind of canary yellow car that somebody gave him a deal on and it was pretty noticeable where he was parking and what he was driving. So I think he's really upgraded."

No kidding, coach. For being named the game's most valuable player, Brady walked away with a loaded black Cadillac Escalade EXT and a trip to Disney World, which is where he went yesterday with his parents, Galynn and Tom Sr. They are due back in Boston today for the parade honoring the Super Bowl champions.

Belichick noted Brady's improvement was not limited to his offseason work. He saw it all season, even before Drew Bledsoe was injured in the second game, opening the door for one of the most unlikely yet remarkable football stories of this or any year.

"I'm not sure I've ever seen any player improve as much as Tom has," Belichick said. "I think that all the accolades and all the success he has had this year, nobody deserves it

more, because nobody worked harder than Tom Brady."

Brady, who had preceded his coach on the dais, was winging it after a night of next-to-no sleep. He said he spent most of the night celebrating at the Fairmont, hobnobbing with people like rapper Snoop Dogg. Brady wore khakis, a dark sweater, a black leather jacket, and a face that, while not expressionless, clearly spoke of a need for rest. "I didn't have a lot of sleep last night, as you can clearly see," Brady joked.

He was introduced by none other than NFL commissioner Paul Tagliabue. The commish noted Brady is the second-youngest MVP; Lynn Swann was younger. The commish did not note that, amazingly, the two went to the same high school: Junipero Serra High in San Mateo, Calif.

Asked about what can only be described as an amazing journey, Brady said, "As far as I'm concerned, it's been straight up. There hasn't been a downer yet, except this morning when the alarm went off at 6 a.m." No, a sleepless night had not dulled his sense of humor.

Brady also drew chuckles when, after being asked a question about why Super Bowl winners with only a week to prepare are usually underdogs, he thought for a second and said,

Doesn't this man look destined for Disney World? Even his coach will tell you that nobody deserves it more.

Brady reminisced about attending games in Candlestick Park as a kid. He was in the stands as a cranky 4-year-old (his parents wouldn't buy him one of those big No. 1 fingers) when Joe Montana connected with Dwight Clark to win the NFC title for the 49ers in 1981. He has a hazy recollection of that game, but a vivid memory of other trips to the stadium to see Montana and Steve Young.

"That's when I realized I wanted to be a football player," he said. "Going into all those games growing up, and I'm glad I chose this as what I wanted to do."

He added he hadn't had enough non-celebratory time to reflect on what he and his team had done. "There might be some time sitting on the beach this week where I can think about it, with a pina colada."

With that, Brady left the podium to take his chartered jet to Disney World.

What more fitting place for him to be. As he chatted amiably outside the conference room with some reporters, his parents also talked about their son.

They've been regulars at every game this season, flying in from California to watch their kismet-sprinkled, hard-working boy. They, too, are caught up in all of it and, like their son, are going with the flow.

"I think it was five or six weeks ago that we just started getting giddy," said Tom Sr. "Everything that happened after that, we just said, 'Thank you, God. Thank you, God. Thank you, God.' None of it came easy to him. He had to fight back. There just aren't enough adjectives to describe what my heart feels." ◆

> "That's when I realized I wanted to be a football player."

"Beats the hell out of me." He also got in some jibes at the slew of writers who predicted an easy Rams win.

"That's what we try to do, to make them [writers] feel stupid," he said. "Actually, some of them do it themselves. Sorry, that was a cheap shot, wasn't it? I take that back. Actually, I won't. You take cheap shots at us."

He was asked if he was prepared for the onslaught of outside opportunities that would likely come his way, starting with yesterday's quick visit to Florida.

"I'm working on it," he cracked. "It's new to me. I'm like a kite in the wind, just kind of going with the flow."

At training camp before the 2002 season, he still carries the glow of having visited the happiest place on earth.

68

2002 SEASON

Adulation

by JACKIE MACMULLAN

September 8, 2002 | He could sense them coming. Tom Brady is alert, and disciplined, so he seldom lowers his head, or leaves himself vulnerable to a blindside hit, because if you relax, lose your focus, they'll converge on you, and corner you, and then that feeling of dread grabs hold, and you're trapped, and a little fearful. You try absorbing a surge of bodies hurtling toward you with that kind of speed and force, knowing there's no place to scramble free.

Ever since basking in the limelight of Boston's Super Bowl celebration, Brady's been the toast of towns all across America. It's heady stuff, but is it also too much too soon?

That's what he gets for trying to grab dinner on a Friday night in public.

"We made the mistake of sitting by a window," said Brady's roommate Dave Nugent, the defensive end who was waived by the Patriots last week. "People were crowded all around us. They were taking pictures, eating our fries. The manager tried to fend them off, but it wasn't working.

"Then there were the people outside, who had their flashes going off through our window. We were getting it from all over the place."

One year earlier, Nugent and Brady dined at the same Chili's, in the same booth, on a similar Friday night. They were regulars at the restaurant, two anonymous kids trying to hook on in the NFL, sharing hopes and dreams of grandeur and glory.

Funny thing about Brady, though. He didn't ponder "if" he'd be a starting quarterback. His dreams always started with when he became a starting quarterback. He studied coach Bill Belichick's playbook so thoroughly, he could recite complete passages. He dissected the game and psyche of Drew Bledsoe, and recorded a mental ledger of pluses and minuses. He spent hours in the weight room, and hours more on agility drills.

He fastidiously prepared himself to be the quarterback of the New England Patriots as if he knew exactly what was about to transpire.

"I know a lot of people are surprised at how well Tom has done," said Donald Yee, Brady's attorney, "but quite frankly, we planned for something just like this."

Who dares to plan for a Super Bowl victory, an MVP trophy, a Pro Bowl selection, and a new contract that's worth 20 times the old one? Tom Brady is not that vain or that arrogant; he didn't map out the tangible rewards of his quest, only the larger picture and its results.

"I always believed I could be a starting quarterback in the NFL," Brady said, "because I knew I was willing to do whatever was required to get there."

His exploding fame has designated him as the multi-tiered symbol for clutch performer, teen idol, football hero, clean-cut icon, and doughnut pitchman.

Winning the Super Bowl? Who would have ever guessed that would be the easy part? It's dealing with the notoriety from his overnight success that's keeping Brady up nights.

"I have changed," said Boston's most dynamic young sports star. "I'm trying to survive. This is a whole new world I'm trying to live in, and I'm still trying to figure it all out."

He remembers the first time he realized he'd crossed the threshold from athlete to celebrity. He and Nugent had finished eating at a Boston-area Outback Steakhouse, and as they strolled toward the exit, the patrons dropped their knives and forks, and spontaneously broke into prolonged applause. They leaped from their seats to give the young quarterback, only 24 years old, a standing ovation.

And the Patriots hadn't even won a playoff game yet.

STAR TREATMENT

Adulation is routine now; incessant, in fact. Brady cannot go to the Outback, the grocery store, the car wash, or his team's lunchroom at Bryant College without confronting a steady stream of requests for an autograph, a picture, a comment, or a story.

"Overwhelmed?" said Brady. "I'm overwhelmed all the time — until I get where I'm most comfortable, on the football field."

He doesn't want to sound ungrateful. He knows you all wish you could be him. Like his father said: it's better than being a fourth-string quarterback nobody has ever heard of.

Besides, the perks of the superstar business are excellent. Brady flew on Donald Trump's private jet, judged a beauty pageant, won an ESPY award, and sat in the front row at some choice concerts. He chatted backstage with country singer John Michael Montgomery. He has mingled with the top entertainers in the world, and has danced with some of the prettiest. "We used to go out to clubs together all the time," Nugent said. "We'd try to talk to girls. We'd tell them, 'We play for the Patriots,' and they'd be like, 'Yeah, sure, whatever.' They wouldn't give Tom the time of day.'"

"It's true," Brady confesses, almost wistfully. "We'd say, 'Hey, we play football,' and they'd say, 'Great. Now get in the back of the line.'"

That was before total strangers proposed to him on the street; before teenage girls drove to his apartment, knocked on the door, and asked him to be their prom date; before a woman, desperate for Brady to notice her, lifted her blouse and exposed herself.

Brady does not know how to process this. He wants to be the same person he was before Feb. 3, when he engineered the final drive to provide championship-starved New England with some new hardware.

His legendary work ethic, the one that kept him engaged in two-a-day workouts in

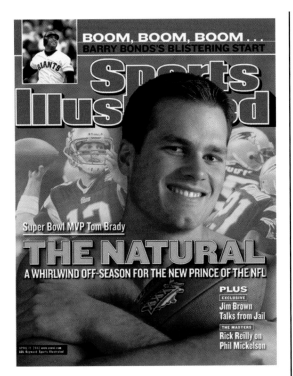

A shirtless Brady appears on the cover of the April 15, 2002 edition of Sports Illustrated, in which the NFL's newest hunk talks about learning to cope with sudden fame.

high school, is not helpful. Brady's solution to thorny problems has always been to work harder. You can't outwork fans. There are simply too many of them.

"It wears you down a little when you can't go to the dry cleaners without signing for a half an hour," Brady acknowledged. "We all have moods and emotions. I'm happy sometimes, and I have bad days, too, but now you wonder if you're allowed any bad days."

Sometimes, when he sees a gaggle of kids coming, he's tempted to turn his heels and run. But then he remembers when he was 10, and he and his buddy were admitted to the roped-off area where the San Francisco 49er players parked their cars.

"I thought it was the greatest thing ever," Brady said. "I was going to be able to walk up to these football players and get their autographs. Now here I am, like them, trying to get to my car as fast as I can.

"Don't get me wrong. Ninety-nine percent of the time, what's happened to me is great. But I guess you start taking the great part for granted, because that other one percent puts so many demands on your time."

When Brady was called upon as an emergency fill-in for the injured Bledsoe last Sept. 23, some of his teammates viewed him warily. Bledsoe was a private man, but he was popular in the locker room, and had earned the respect of his peers. Some of the veterans withheld judgment on Brady until they were sure: was this kid, who spurned interviews with Elle magazine and Rolling Stone for Boys Life, the real deal?

"For me, [he answered it] during the Pittsburgh [AFC championship] game," Lawyer Milloy said. "We went down there a day early together to do interviews. It was obvious at that point our team wasn't getting any respect.

"We started having a conversation about the type of adversity we both had to deal with early in our careers. By the time we were done talking, I realized I was talking to a fierce competitor.

"I felt good knowing there was someone like that on the other side of the ball."

ULTRA COMPETITIVE

Brady has taken great pains to try to remain one of the guys. He refused to go to the interview room postgame, preferring to do his business at his locker, alongside his peers. He emphasizes "we" whenever he can. He tells people he'd never want to be Tiger Woods, because when he wins, who can he share it with? They are nice sentiments, all of them, but you can't alter the facts. Tom Brady is the only superstar roaming the new Gillette Stadium.

"Tom is going to get all the accolades," Milloy said. "The quarterback always does. I believe I deserve as much money as he does, but that's

An aerial view of the Super Bowl XXXVI victory rally at Boston's City Hall Plaza shows a fraction of the adoring public that Brady can't escape. Not that he's complaining.

not how football works. We understand that. It doesn't matter. Tom has to go out and be Tom. If he does, we'll all be happy. It's not hard to keep Tom Brady grounded. What you see is what you get." What the Patriots have gotten is a polite, young gentleman in public, and a fiercely intense football player in the huddle.

"He focused so hard on each game, when the Super Bowl ended, he was still saying, 'OK, who do we take on next?'" said his father, Tom Brady Sr. "He has this incredible ability to zero in, and once he's got that tunnel vision, he can't see anything else."

His teammates quickly identified their quarterback's thirst for perfection. Receiver David Patten recalled a scrimmage last fall when Brady threw back-to-back incomplete passes, then slammed his helmet in disgust. "I thought to myself, 'Wow, this kid really wants to win,'" said Patten. Patten witnessed that same competitiveness in training camp, when rookie Deion Branch whipped Brady in a game of ping-pong.

"It wasn't that big of a deal," said Patten, "but Tom walked around the rest of the day saying, 'I can't believe I let that kid beat me.'" He spent the better part of the next day at the ping-pong table.

When he was a kid, and thought he'd be a baseball player, Brady spent hours at the batting cage, refining his swing. When he took up football, and his coach told him he needed to improve his foot speed, he spent so much time developing jump rope techniques that the staff adopted many of them for camp.

After Brady's junior season in high school, his coach, Tom MacKenzie, called him into his office. "We were considering nominations for all-league," said MacKenzie. "Our coaching staff looked at Tom's statistics, and they were very credible. But the truth was we thought he was capable of so much more. We felt it was giving him the wrong message to nominate him when we knew he could do better.

"I'm sure Tom was disappointed when we told him. But, if he was, he did a wonderful job of hiding it."

Perhaps that's because Brady had never been handed anything. When he was a kid, his father pummeled him in golf, darts, and pool. If the kid won on his own, then fine, but Dad had no plans to take it easy on him.

No wonder when Brady learned last winter he was headed for the Pro Bowl, he was actually crestfallen. "My first reaction was, 'Aw, c'mon, let me earn it,'" Brady explained. "It was too much too soon. I hopefully have a long career ahead of me. Getting all this stuff so early... sometimes it worries me. I've always had to work hard for everything I've ever gotten. Things don't usually come easy for me."

It wasn't easy to report to Michigan as the sixth quarterback on the depth chart. It wasn't easy to win the starting job, then watch your coach make you split time with another kid, Drew Henson, who was threatening to play pro baseball, and demanded more playing time on the football field.

Henson and Brady split quarterback duties for a few weeks, until it was clear Brady was the better choice. He went on to have a terrific senior season as the Wolverines' undisputed No. 1 passer. "I learned from it," said Brady. "When I was in college, I compared myself to other guys. I'd spend all day saying, 'He does this, but I do that better. Why does he get time when I do this?' It was an immature approach to competition."

When he became the No. 1 quarterback in New England, Brady understood the importance of conveying confidence. The only way

> "Getting all this stuff so early ... worries me. I've always had to work hard for everything I've ever gotten."

he would convince his team he could handle the job was to demonstrate his superior preparation, and his belief in himself.

"His demeanor has always been the same," said offensive lineman Damien Woody. "He was a great leader from the first time he walked into the huddle and took the snap. That's the great thing about Tom. He hasn't changed at all."

Woody is wrong. Tom Brady has changed, and his life will never be the same. For the first time in eight years, he didn't take a vacation with his father this summer. The constraints of his packed schedule prevented it.

Brady has taken steps to simplify his life. He has declined television appearances on the "The Tonight Show with Jay Leno" and "Good Morning America." He has politely refused most personal appearances.

The list of endorsements he has rejected is impressive. Yee refuses to divulge the companies involved, but the potential endorsements included a major fast-food chain, a soft drink, grooming products, financial services companies, and car companies.

"Doing commercials takes a tremendous amount of time and energy," Yee said. "Tom and I both agreed the most important thing for him was to stay as fresh as possible for the football season, and that meant limiting his activities off the field."

Brady did sign with Dunkin' Donuts, a company with a strong New England presence that also happens to be a major sponsor of the Patriots. Ironically, one of the television spots for Dunkin' Donuts features Brady trading uniforms with a security guard so he can eat his breakfast sandwich in peace. Oh, if only shedding his skin was that simple.

"We went to the movies this summer," Nugent said. "Tom wanted to see 'The Sum of All

> ## "The only thing I fear is not living up to my own expectations."

Fears.' He had his hat pulled down so far over his head he couldn't see a damn thing. He was bumping into poles, and walls, and people. But I told him I was proud of him. He's got to live his life."

Brady's life now includes cars with tinted windows, caller ID, a new condo (don't ask where — we're not telling), and a bucketful of sunglasses and hats.

"I used to go to Red Sox games and sit on the third base line," Brady said. "If I tried to do that now, it wouldn't be the same, so I've got to figure out other ways I can go with my friends and enjoy myself."

He has learned to arrive in darkness when he goes home to visit his parents, otherwise neighbors line up across his family's lawn when they see him approach the house.

"I have a benefits business," said Tom Brady Sr. "I'm in the relationship business, really. I have hundreds of clients, and they all asked me for my son's autograph. Tom certainly signed his share, but then one day he said, 'Dad, my family has to be my sanctuary. I'm public property in Boston. I need to have someplace to be myself.'"

Nugent claims his roommate's biggest fear, in the wake of all the attention, is to be "a one-hit wonder," but quickly adds it will never happen, because Brady works far too hard.

"The only thing I fear is not living up to my own expectations," countered Brady. "I've seen guys who have had a year of success, or three years of success, but what I'm looking for is consistency over my career. I've followed Steve Young, Joe Montana, John Elway, Dan Marino, and every year those guys were at the top."

He knows little will suffice for a suitable encore to last season's storybook ride, but he's confident he's a better player. He's more aware of the timing of the plays, the speed of

When Brady arrived at training camp in 2001 (above left), the only fan around was the one he carried in along with his luggage. But in 2002, after his head-spinning rise to Super Bowl MVP status, Brady comes to camp (above) with everyone wanting a piece of him.

the game, the need to act quickly. Coach Bill Belichick has allowed him more input into the play calling. "You don't go from being a good player to a great player in three weeks — probably not even in three years," Brady said. "The hardest thing is to be patient."

He has already enhanced his role as a team leader. He was always talkative, but now that voice exudes just a bit more authority.

"You sense Tom stepping up a little more and telling everyone, 'This is my team,'" said Patten. "He's more vocal. He doesn't hesitate to say, 'Hey, you ran that route wrong.'"

There's a fine line between being a superstar, and acting like one. Brady's biggest challenge has been to walk that line with his teammates. "He's been great with everyone," said receiver Troy Brown. "It seems like everyone on this team has a kid, a nephew, a niece, or a sister that wants to meet Tom Brady, or have him sign a ball, or have their picture taken with

him. Believe me, it goes on and on. But sometimes you have to tell people, 'You know what? I'm tired of this.'"

Brady's safe house is the football field, where he is rarely blindsided by anything. He knows repeating is a monumental task, particularly with an offensive line that was shuffled in the exhibition season because of injuries. But he's already focused his attention on a seemingly insurmountable goal: to up the ante on last year's dream season.

"That's just the way competitive people are," Brady said. "I never feel like I've reached the top. There's always this feeling I've got something left to push for."

This much is true: if the New England Patriots win back-to-back Super Bowls, there won't be a restaurant in New England that will be able to guarantee the quarterback any privacy. ♦

Above left: The Vince Lombardi Trophy, awarded to the New England Patriots for winning Super Bowl XXXVI.

Above right: Brady never makes much of his injuries, but here he's seen stretching an arm that seems to be causing some discomfort during the final game of the season, even if it isn't enough to keep him on the sidelines.

Sophomore Slump

by RON BORGES

December 31, 2002 | Bill Parcells may believe "You are what you are," but apparently one of his disciples doesn't. At least not 24 hours after his team had been eliminated from play-off contention.

"I know what the record says," Patriots coach Bill Belichick said of his 9-7 team that ended its season Sunday with a stirring overtime win over the Miami Dolphins but a disappointing elimination hours later when the New York Jets won the AFC East title by destroying the Green Bay Packers.

"It looks like a roller coaster, but I don't know that I saw that week to week the way some other people did. I didn't see it in terms of the team's work ethic and performance. I just didn't see the roller coaster some others did."

Actually, Belichick had a good point, although not likely the one he thought he was making. The Patriots, who became the 10th team to miss the playoffs the year after winning the Super Bowl, started 3-1 after Belichick's "Targeting September" campaign, then went 1-3, followed by 3-1, before ending 2-2 with two losses in the final three weeks. That might seem to be a roller coaster but in fact Belichick's Patriots were far more a picture of consistency. Unfortunately, what they were consistent at was not being competitive against the NFL's best teams.

By the end of the season, New England had not beaten a team that will be in the playoffs since Sept. 15, when they defeated a far different Jets team than the one that dismantled them, 30-17, on Dec. 22. Overall, they went 3-6 against teams that finished with a winning record — 1-6 after opening with victories over Pittsburgh and the Jets that appeared to many to launch New England into the NFL's stratosphere.

In the end, the Patriots would come crashing down to earth, but the process began long before most people noticed the dry rot at the foundation of the team. It surfaced, Belichick finally acknowledged yesterday, in a Week 3 victory over the Kansas City Chiefs in which Priest Holmes ran over them for 180 yards, averaging 6 yards per carry.

"In that Kansas City game, we got exposed on some things," Belichick said. "We saw some things that were definitely a problem and they continued to be a problem."

The biggest problem was that after failing to improve their defense even though all but one starter returned from the Super Bowl team, the Patriots were not stout enough in the middle to stop any superior runner and were not fast enough on the outside to keep them from running wide as well.

What resulted was a unit that finished 31st

79

(out of 32 teams) in rushing defense, ending the year fittingly by allowing 256 rushing yards to the Dolphins, an average of 6.9 yards per carry.

As Belichick looked back on the season, he wisely noted that he would take several weeks off before making any long-term decisions about the team, but he could not ignore a glaring fact in the stark reality of having utterly failed in his effort to defend the Super Bowl title.

"We have the oldest team in the league on defense," Belichick said. "We've got to try and infuse a little youth into that group. Age on defense is an issue for us."

Age is not the only issue, however. So, too, is the approach the organization has taken in free agency the past two offseasons. The Patriots spent little money and much time looking for cheap help, basically rent-a-players in the latter stages of their careers. Belichick tried to rewrite his history in that area yesterday, insisting, "There seems to be a conception, or rather a misconception, that we won't sign a player who makes a certain amount of money."

If you can think of a high-profile free agent Belichick has paid much beyond the minimum level, you would be among the few NFL observers able to do so. In fact, only minutes after Belichick tried to make the point that he was no Scrooge when it came to veteran free agents, he seemed to argue against his own point when he added, "If they can do it for the value, we're interested. That being said, if you don't have significant cap space, which we haven't, and you don't have the resources, you don't consider them. Our policy is to take an open mind but you have to be realistic, too."

In other words, the misconception he spoke about seems to be a lot less of one after the signing of 13 guys out of Filene's Basement and the netting of one starter last offseason despite having significantly more cap space than the previous year.

Belichick was asked if his team had put too much pressure on the shoulders of quarterback Tom Brady, who in only his second season as a starter was asked to throw 601 times, fourth-most in team history, while the offense rushed only 395 times, the third-lowest total in club history since the 16-game season began in 1978.

The offense was utterly out of balance and, according to Jets defensive lineman Jason Ferguson, quite predictable by the end of the season. In the second meeting, New York limited the Patriots' offense to 216 total yards and only 119 yards passing.

By comparison, when they were going 14-5 a year ago, the Patriots threw 482 times and ran the ball 473. Historically, balanced attacks have been the most effective in the NFL, yet Belichick and offensive coordinator Charlie Weis abandoned that concept after averaging more than 300 passing yards a game in the first month of the season.

Things never got back into balance, even when Brady's production fell off markedly as the season progressed. As defenses began to tighten down on New England's short, lateral passing game after deciding Brady could not challenge them deep and the Patriots' running game would not challenge them at all, the quarterback's production predictably began to suffer.

Brady passed for fewer than 240 yards in each of the final seven games and in three of the last four threw for fewer than 200, averaging only 168.5 in the final month — at a time when New England desperately needed to win to stay alive for the playoffs. The wisdom of relying on a young quar-

> Brady passed for fewer than 240 yards in each of the final seven games.

QB12 and his offensive coordinator, Charlie Weis, share a dejected moment on the bench late in the fourth quarter of a 28-10 loss to the Green Bay Packers.

terback's production seemed particularly suspect when one considers that while Brady's 28 touchdown passes tied his predecessor Drew Bledsoe for second-best in Patriot history, only seven of them came in the team's seven losses.

Brady threw 21 touchdown passes and only five interceptions in New England's nine victories, including 11 TDs against defensive weak sisters Chicago, Buffalo, and Minnesota, but had only seven touchdowns and nine interceptions in the losses. Brady threw only one touchdown pass in the final three defeats of the season, games that ultimately finished off the Patriots' playoff hopes. In pro football, teams that try to live

Far left: For the fourth straight game, things don't go the right way for Brady and the rest of the New England Patriots as they fall at home to the Denver Broncos 24-16, dropping to 3-4 on the season.

Above: Brady chases down a mishandled snap during a 41-38 dogfight with the Kansas City Chiefs. He then fires an incomplete pass to avoid any loss of yardage. The Patriots win, barely.

Left: Maybe he's grasping at straws, but the quarterback adjusts his new gloves during practice.

by the pass generally die by it, and that was the fate of Belichick's philosophy, one that drifted far away from what it had been only a year ago when his was among the most balanced offenses in football.

"That's something to look at," Belichick conceded when asked about whether he had asked his quarterback to throw too much. "It's probably something to look at." But before Belichick will look at anything, he said he would take a step or two back.

"It's good to step back and wipe the slate clean to address the season as a whole and your team as a whole and not based on one specific game," Belichick said.

"It's more important to look at the games the team didn't do well in. What were the problems? To find out, we have to look at the seven games we lost."

When he does, Belichick will have to admit two things: He has serious personnel problems in a lot of areas - not only his aging defense but also along the offensive line — and his offensive approach will have to be adjusted.

The first question that must be answered is whether Belichick can admit, at least to himself, his own mistakes in judgment this season or whether he will continue to say, as he did yesterday, "Our football team all felt there were other games that were winnable for us. But we didn't win them."

No, they didn't, and every team that's out of the playoffs today is whistling the same tune. A bounce here, a call there, a play someplace else, and everything would be different, they're all saying this morning.

The leaders of the teams who ultimately can admit that it was more than that may not have to repeat that speech next December. The ones who refuse usually get to say the same words next year — often while packing. ♦

Weary

by BOB RYAN

December 30, 2002 | Here's some free and utterly unsolicited advice for Tom Brady: Go home and go to bed.

Sleep for a day. Sleep for two days. Sleep for a week. Whatever it takes.

And when you finally wake up, vegetate. Order takeout. Read a book. Read 10 books. Watch everything AMC, TMC, Bravo, and HBO have to offer. Watch no playoffs. Treat football like some arcane academic discipline you wouldn't get yourself involved in if you lived to be 437, or had decided to join The Thumper in that Arizona freezer.

Please draw the curtain. The Super Bowl, its aftermath, the First Season of the Rest of Your Life, and any attendant fallout from the events of late 2001 and the first 34 days of 2002 are now part of your history. You did what you did, and no one can take any of it from you. But it has been one endless stretch of activity and pressure. You have pushed yourself to the max, physically and mentally. You need a complete and thorough rest. And you know it, too.

"I feel tired," Brady admitted. "It's been a long season."

But it wasn't long enough.

The Patriots did what they had to do yesterday, coming from 11 points behind in the final 4:54 to tie the game before defeating the Miami Dolphins in overtime, 27-24. It was the first great happening in their new stadium, and it gave everyone who witnessed it, not to mention the Patriots themselves, a temporary warm-and-fuzzy feeling. It still wasn't enough to get them into the playoffs, because some 225 miles to the south the despised New York Jets were doing what they had to do, blasting their way into the playoffs via a 42-17 mauling of the Green Bay Packers. Part A of this parlay wasn't going to have any lasting meaning for the Patriots without Part B. The Patriots had to win and the Jets had to lose. But the Jets came up big.

When he was most needed, Brady likewise came up big. The Patriots were trailing, 24-13, when Brady got the ball back with 4:54 remaining and drove them 68 yards in 10 plays for a touchdown. There was a lot of that dink-and-dunk paper-cutting for which he has become famous, but there was also a vital 20-yard connection with David Patten, as well as a somewhat fortuitous 30-yard pass interference gain (it sure looked more like an offensive, rather than a defensive, infraction) that put the ball on the Miami 3 and set up a touchdown pass to Troy Brown two plays later. A 2-point conversion pass to Christian Fauria (serious props for a great leaping/falling backward catch in the back of the end zone) made it a 24-21 game.

No Brady heroics were needed to get Adam Vinatieri in position for the tying field goal, since the defense handed the ball back at the Miami 34 and Kevin Faulk made the key play, a 9-yard run to the 25. But Brady made a great throw in the OT, drilling one on the

Wide receiver Troy Brown gets a thanks from his teammate after a touchdown pass in the late stages of a thrilling Dec. 29 comeback win over Miami. It's too little too late for the Patriots' playoff hopes, but a nice way to go out.

right sideline to Faulk, who made a four-star grab for a 20-yard gain to the Dolphins 25. For a little insurance, Brady threw a 7-yarder to Brown.

After that, it was simply a matter of calling on the ultra-reliable Vinatieri, who knocked home the 35-yard winner. "Adam is as clutch as there is in football," Brady said. "I mean, there is never a [thought], when I go out, when I am running off the field with him coming on, that he is going to miss it."

It was a game that had Last Year written all over it, with Brady putting up unspectacular numbers (25 for 44, 221 yards, one TD, and one interception), even as he seemed to loom larger and larger as the game wore on. Until such time as he is gifted with a more stable offensive line, better receivers, and/or has a Grade A running back to work with, as opposed to the earnest but limited Antowain Smith, no one ever will know how good Brady can be. Right now, he plays with the hand that has been dealt, and he makes the most of it.

He is a team guy, for sure, and he never will admit publicly that it has been a hard year, one in which he took a lot of tough shots. In fact, he may have been playing hurt yesterday (analyst Phil Simms wondered aloud about that during the NBC telecast), and it looked as if he might have been favoring his right shoulder or wrist. He was uncommonly long in the trainer's room after the game. True to The Code, he would give only name, rank, and serial number when the subject was broached by the ever-prying media.

"What injury?" he smiled. "I am always hurt after games. I feel good. We won the game. I feel good about that."

When pressed, he 'fessed up to "bumps and bruises," but nothing more. Nor would he locate said owies. "It is fine, it is fine," he insisted. "Not a big deal."

Fine. Brady has earned the right to have it his way. Of course, he is extremely disappointed that his season is over. Alluding to a talk the quarterbacks had Saturday morning, Brady said his take was "I'm not ready for this season to end."

But now that it is over, Brady can admit that enough is enough. "These weeks go on, and I think a lot of times in the end of the year a lot of guys are just playing, you know, you are just playing on the vapor," he said, "You know, there is no gas in the tank left."

Any number of his teammates are far more banged up than Brady. But no one else on this team has been living the hybrid life of championship athlete and mega-celebrity to the extent Brady has, and he needs a major battery recharge.

This season was an unbroken extension of last season, but now the entire Super Bowl thing is over. The Patriots officially have become the immediate past champions now, and it is time for Tom Brady to crash.

So listen up, kid. Go home. Get out of our sight. We'll see you when we see you, OK? ♦

He's not phoning home, but he is getting help – from Patriots personnel who are busy dissecting every move made on the field.

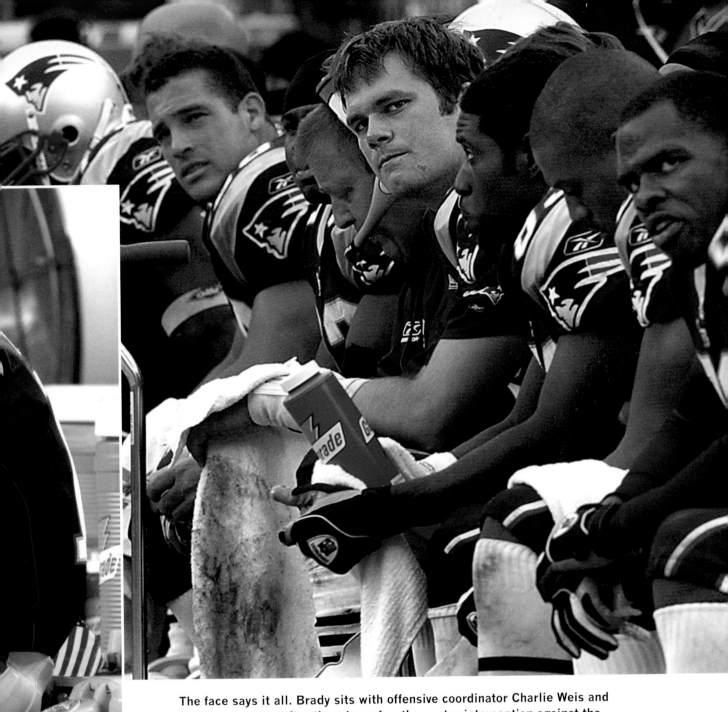

The face says it all. Brady sits with offensive coordinator Charlie Weis and other teammates after throwing a fourth-quarter interception against the Green Bay Packers. That turnover contributes to a Patriots loss, 28-10.

2003 SEASON

Recharge

by JACKIE MACMULLAN

September 7, 2003 | To measure progress, you must gauge advancement toward a goal or a higher purpose. Can you now see Tom Brady's quandary? His pilgrimage began at the pinnacle. The fervent wish of any professional football player is to win a Super Bowl ring; Brady completed that quest on his very first attempt.

The letdown after such a whirlwind journey is predictable; so, too, is the inevitable tearing down of the icon. The Patriots were casualties of their own lofty status last season, catching no one unaware and looking entirely mortal in the trudge through a 9-7 campaign.

The quarterback, the overnight poster boy sensation, easily could have been targeted to absorb the wrath of disappointed fans, who at the very least expected a repeat playoff appearance. But Brady's numbers were, in some instances, even better than the year he was declared invincible. He threw for more yards (3,764), more touchdowns (28) — and yes, two more interceptions (14) — while his completion percentage dipped only slightly, from 63.9 to 62.1.

"Even though the team didn't do as well, Brady may have been better," said Buffalo Bills general manager Tom Donahoe, whose team faces the Patriots today in the season

It's a new day, with cause for a well-dressed high five from team owner Robert Kraft following New England's 31-10 victory over Philadelphia on Sept. 14.

opener. "Some of that is just maturity. He's developing into a very good quarterback. He's extremely competitive, and, from the outside looking in, seems to be very popular with his teammates. And he knows where to go with the ball. He doesn't make many mistakes."

Year 3 of the quarterback's journey kicks off today with Brady and his team no longer at the pinnacle. They tumbled down the mountain long ago, regrouping as a collection of foot soldiers preparing for the grueling trek back up the hill. No bull's-eyes were needed on the back of their jerseys in this summer's exhibition games. The Patriots are just another football team again, although Brady is not just another quarterback.

"He's got it," said Charley Armey, general manager of the St. Louis Rams. "When I look back on the Super Bowl tape, I'm impressed with his poise and his confidence. No matter how well a guy does in college, you can never be sure how well he'll do at our level, because of the speed of the game. Brady has the patience to deal with it. He bought into a system the Patriots devised for him, and he has functioned within that system at a high level."

As the quarterback grows, he yearns to expand that offensive system, to test his maturity on the field. He has already been tested in his personal life by an avalanche of publicity that obliterated any fleeting hopes of occasional anonymity. Brady no longer needs a police escort to drop off his dry cleaning, but he may never be able to wander into a movie theater uninterrupted again.

"I'm more comfortable with finding ways to get things accomplished," said Brady. "When I look back on that [Super Bowl] year, in a lot of ways I was still very young. I'm not saying I'm the sage old veteran now, but I feel older. You've got to grow up quickly. This job demands it."

REALITY CHECK

The sobering release of Lawyer Milloy for salary cap purposes last week only cemented Brady's belief that football is all about business. He saw that first-hand when coach Bill Belichick promised an injured Drew Bledsoe that he'd have his job when he returned, only to change his mind when Brady led the team on a winning streak. Loyalty, says Brady, is simply not compatible with the NFL.

"I think it's OK to think that way," Brady said. "I learned a tough lesson coming out of Michigan [where Drew Henson encroached on his status as the No. 1 quarterback]. I thought I was owed something. That wasn't the way it was.

"I'll never forget that. I'll always work, so at least at the end of the day I can say, no matter what happens, that I did my part. I can

> "He bought into a system the Patriots devised for him, and he has functioned within that system at a high level."

sleep at night. I might not like the outcome, but I'll believe in myself. I'm sure Lawyer still believes in himself."

Belichick's hard-line stances are legendary, and forecasters have already predicted that Ty Law will be gone at the end of the season. Brady, by virtue of the confidence the coach has exhibited in him, is considered immune from the bottom-line mentality. The quarterback says he knows better.

"I'm [Belichick's] guy until we lose some games," said Brady, on the day Milloy was released. "I'm no dummy. I know everybody is going to treat you one way on the way up, but it's going to be the other way when you're coming down."

He was unprepared for the adulation that enveloped him as the Super Bowl season unfolded, and found it to be both exhilarating and exhausting. "After we won the Super Bowl, I was down at the Pro Bowl thinking, 'I'm so tired. Get me out of here,'" Brady said. "It was too bad I felt that way. That's when it hit me that I couldn't do everything. I couldn't make everybody happy. And I couldn't do it all alone."

The Pro Bowl did turn out to be useful. Surrounded by some of the best players in football, Brady took mental notes of their specific talents.

"Rich Gannon was in the game, and he had mirror receivers on both sides," said Brady. "He did a three-step drop back, and was looking to throw the ball to the slant [receiver]. He looked right, pump-faked, and jumped to the left and threw the ball without ever looking over there. He put the ball in Marvin Harrison's hands, and Harrison ran 60 yards for a touchdown.

"When he came over to the sidelines, I said, 'Rich, how did you do that? What were you looking at?' He said, 'Well, I've run that play a lot of times now.'"

Brady cannot fast-forward to gain more experience, nor can he acquire it in film sessions, strategy meetings, or offseason workouts. He has no choice but to patiently wait, listen, learn, and adjust. His coach said the difference from Year 1 to Year 3 has been a subtle process of acquired information.

"Tom is the type of player that rather than see one thing in his game that jumps significantly from here to there, he might have 10 different things that improve incrementally," Belichick said.

Opponents have singled out Brady's ability to identify defenses as his most improved area.

"He wasn't as sure of himself in the pocket as he is now," Donahoe said. "He's just a lot more poised."

"That Super Bowl year, if you remember, he had one day where he had something like four interceptions in the Denver game," said Armey. "They were heavily blitzing him. That kind of coverage doesn't bother him so much anymore. Now he's got good sight adjustment in the huddle.

"That might be one of the things I like most about Brady. If he sees something at the line, he's mentally quick enough to bring the ball down and eat it, or throw it away, instead of letting something really bad happen to the offense."

LONG AND SHORT OF IT

As the quarterback blossoms, a nagging question lingers. Brady's detractors remain unconvinced that he has the talent to throw the long pass. Asked about this persistent criticism, and if he thought a bigger, taller receiver would quell some of the criticism, Brady answered, "Sure, it would be great to have a big receiver. And I'm sure my receivers would like a guy who can run around back there and buy them time to get open, too."

Pressed to address his ability to execute the deep patterns, Brady responded, "Well, if it's not one thing, it's another. Can I throw the long ball? Hell, yeah. Have I shown it? Not to my liking. It's one of the many things I'm working on."

Armey said such criticism is unfounded.

"First of all, he has enough arm strength to throw the long ball," said Armey. "And second of all, arm strength is the most overrated thing in football. Accuracy, getting the ball off on time, and getting it to the right person is what matters.

"All I know is that pass he threw on the last drive to win the Super Bowl looked like a pretty good long ball to me."

As Brady tries to bring his team back to the playoffs, he has cut down on some of his appearances and endorsements. He has never, he insists, allowed any of his extracurricular activities to interfere with football.

"I've been around a lot of players at this point," said Patriots owner Robert Kraft, "and I've seen the sense of celebrity ruin them. The demands on Tom have been quite extensive, but he's learned how to handle it. He hasn't fallen into the trap of believing his own celebrity. He hasn't allowed himself to be intoxicated by it."

Once in a while, Brady drifts back to a time before this incredible journey began, when he was another fresh-faced backup quarterback who tried to meet girls by telling them he played for the Patriots. Many times, the ladies would roll their eyes and move on. Now they send him marriage proposals in the mail.

"I don't like what some of this has done," Brady said. "I feel so out of touch with my family sometimes. I mean, I still talk to them 2-3 times a week, but I used to talk to them every day and for a while there I was lucky if I checked in with them once a week. At that point, you start saying, 'What am I doing?'"

Year 3 for the quarterback features a new young linebacker in Rosevelt Colvin, a new fullback (Larry Centers) who likes to catch passes, a hot young receiver (Bethel John-

"You've got to grow up quickly. This job demands it," says Brady. Yeah, but nobody minds if you still look like a kid having fun.

son) who can really move, Milloy would have been starting.

"If there's one thing you take out of it, it's you better be aware every single day," said Brady. "And even when you are aware, something could still happen. If you start getting a big ego, and thinking you are the be-all and end-all, you're not safe. No one is safe."

Not even the quarterback who grabbed the brass ring on the very first try. ♦

Chasing Montana

by MICHAEL SMITH

January 7, 2004 | Here's why the comparisons to Joe Montana don't work. Yet.

Joe Theismann won one Super Bowl. So did Jim McMahon. And Phil Simms. And Doug Williams. Jeff Hostetler. Mark Rypien. Trent Dilfer. Brad Johnson. Tom Brady is closer to that group than he is to Montana. For now.

Here's why the comparisons to Montana will work. Soon. Perhaps by Feb. 2.

Brady's career is just beginning. He's already the youngest quarterback in league history to win a Super Bowl, having done so at 24 years, 184 days old. Before Brady, Montana and Joe Namath were the youngest at 25 years 227 days. Brady has as many postseason starts as Montana has Super Bowl MVP trophies. For now.

That's why there's a little extra pep in Brady's step this week. That's why he stares at the Super Bowl XXXVI MVP trophy that sits by his bedside. This is his season. The postseason. It was two years ago in the playoffs

Above: Even commanding the Chiefs in 1993, Montana could still sling it.

Left: Looking downfield for an open receiver, Brady strikes a Montana-esque pose with the pigskin.

that Brady went from being a story to a star overnight.

"I want another [title]," Brady told ESPN The Magazine for its Jan. 19 issue. "Can you imagine? Two Super Bowls?"

Then we can talk. Maybe even about Brady and Montana in the same conversation, sans the qualifiers. Right now it's not even close.

"They're both right-handed quarterbacks," Bill Belichick said. "You're talking about Joe Montana. The guy is a Hall of Fame quarterback. He's won however many Super Bowls he's won. How many guys can you compare to him?"

Brady, maybe?

He was "Joe Cool" cool in his first postseason appearance two years ago, right up until the spike to stop the clock for Adam Vinatieri's championship-clinching kick. He's been clutch in this, his third year as a starter, finishing third in league MVP voting after leading the Patriots to the league's best record and home-field advantage throughout the playoffs, which for them begin Saturday night at Gillette Stadium against the Tennessee Titans. If New England wins its second title in three years, Brady already will be halfway to Montana.

"He's the best of all time," Brady said yesterday. "Joe Montana, he was everything. Everything that he did was great. He threw the ball great. He managed his game great. He made his other players great. He really had some great qualities. I think as a quarterback you have to emulate some of those things.

"There will never be another Joe Montana. Can guys do some of those things? [Dan] Marino could throw the ball great. [John] Elway could improvise great. Do I think I have any of those great qualities? I'm working at it. I'm working to try to become that, but it's going to have to take a lot more playoff games and a lot more Super Bowl wins to ever mention those two names in the same sentence."

Mention the postseason to Brady, and you see in his face what his teammates see when they're looking back at him in the huddle in the fourth quarter: It.

"These are the type of weeks that in February and March and April and May you just think about," he said. "What greater of an opportunity could you ever have than to be a starting quarterback in this game?"

Hard to believe it's been almost two years since Brady's first playoff start, Jan. 19, 2002, against Oakland at Foxboro Stadium. No one on the team remembers seeing seeing any nervousness in Brady during the two weeks leading up to the game. "The same as he was the week before," Belichick recalled yesterday. "The same as he was going into Carolina. The same as he was going into Miami. The same as he was going into whoever we played before Miami that year, the Jets, I can't even remember [Buffalo]."

Brady went into the Raiders game unproven in the playoffs. He came out of it a local legend, having rallied the Patriots from a 13-3 deficit after three quarters by passing for 138 yards in the fourth and overtime — with a little help, of course, from the "tuck" rule.

Brady established Patriots postseason passing records in that game for attempts (52), completions (32), and passing yards (312). He also ran for a touchdown. He hit on 26 of 39 passes in the second half for 238 yards after he and his teammates were booed off the field at the end of the first half when they trailed, 7-0.

"One thing about Tom is, he's smart, he prepares very hard, and he's resilient," said Belichick, who took the liberty to add two things. "Pressure doesn't really bother him. He is, I think, pretty much unaffected by the score or the situation, the field position, the crowd noise, what happened the play before, all of those things. I think that he has the good ability to put those in the background and focus on what's in front of him."

Or who's above him.

Brady isn't quite on Montana's level. Yet. But give him time. (How's three weeks?) ◆

"Joe Montana, he was everything. Everything that he did was great. ... I think as a quarterback you have to emulate some of those things."

Above: He's no Wilt the Stilt, but Brady – more like Bill Russell – always comes up a winner.

Left: "We'd tell Tom, 'Tell the rest of these rookies that if they're late we're going to move that meeting back to 6 a.m. Let 'em know that.' And after that they were all on time." – Coach Belichick, on Brady's early leadership skills

Just Win

by DAN SHAUGHNESSY

January 16, 2004 | We are old Boston sports fans and we have been down this path before.

We had Bill Russell.

They had Wilt Chamberlain.

Russell did all the little things necessary to win. He'd block a shot and keep it inbounds so he could ignite the fast break. He didn't worry about scoring points. He made his teammates better. He was cool under pressure. He always won.

Wilt was so good it was frightening. He had sheer power and indomitable skills. He averaged 50 points a game and scored 100 in a single night. But he couldn't win the big one. Russell and Red Auerbach were always in his head.

Say hello to Tom Brady and Peyton Manning, starting quarterbacks of Sunday's AFC Championship game. In case you haven't figured it out, Brady is Russell and Manning is Chamberlain. Oh, and Bill Belichick - he's Red.

Like Wilt, Manning is more fun to watch. He throws the deep ball. He hits his wideouts in stride with perfect spirals.

But our guy is better. He's not as much fun to watch, but he's more efficient. Brady couldn't beat Manning in a Punt, Pass & Kick Competition, QB compulsory figures, the long toss, or the indiscernible quarterback ratings, but he is the one you want on your side Sunday afternoon. And he's the biggest reason why the Patriots are going to the Super Bowl and the Colts are not.

Go back to last weekend. Co-MVP/Pro Bowler Steve McNair came to town. His completion percentage and yardage were slightly better than Brady's. But he lost. This weekend the other co-MVP/Pro Bowler is coming to the Razor. No doubt Manning will throw for more yards than Brady. But Brady will win. He almost always wins. Including playoff games, the Patriots are 38-12 with Tom Brady as their starting QB.

Two-and-a-half years after the fact, it's still an incredible story. Brady was a sixth-round pick, the 199th player selected in the 2000 draft. Manning was selected 198 picks earlier in 1998.

Yesterday Belichick hopped into the Wayback Machine and told us a little of what he saw in the young QB who threw a total of three passes in his rookie season.

"Well, he won in college, and the way he handled himself his rookie year, even though he was a lot of times the fourth quarterback, was good. We had a big rookie class of rookies and free agents and they ran their plays after practice and I thought he did a good job that year of taking control of that group. If things weren't going well or we wanted something done, you could say, 'Tom, I want you to take care of this with the rest of these guys' and it pretty well got taken care of . . . Like if one or two rookies were late for the meeting, then we'd tell Tom, 'Tell the rest of these rookies that if they're late we're going to move that meeting back to 6 a.m. Let 'em know that.' And after that they were all on time. I don't know how they got there, but they were there.

"I thought he made a lot of improvement

from his first year to his second year and in training camp he was competing for the second spot. He ended up winning that and had an opportunity to play at the end of the Jet game. It was a progression. I don't think it was any one moment or one play or one throw that did it, but I think it was a lot of hard work in the weight room, the film room, and a lot of execution on the practice field that led to a higher level of performance.

"Ted Marchibroda [former Baltimore Colts coach] told me a long time ago, my first year in the league, that it's better to be prepared and never have the opportunity than to have the opportunity and not be prepared. I think there's a lot of truth to that. You do all you can to be prepared and then when the opportunity strikes, if you are prepared you'll be able to take advantage of it."

OK, Bill. Let's do the "It's a Wonderful Life" drill: What happens if Mo Lewis doesn't make that hit on Drew Bledsoe in the second game of the 2001-02 season? What if there'd been no obvious "opportunity" for Brady to play? Would Foxborough be Pottersville?

"Who knows what would have happened," answered the coach. "You can't predict what's going to happen in this game or in this league. All I know is what did happen. Those are the events that led him to being prepared in that position and then the opportunity presented itself."

And now the Patriots have the guy who hasn't thrown an interception in nine home games. They have the guy who never makes a dumb throw or takes a dumb penalty. They have the 26-year-old guy who's already won a Super Bowl, who never loses his cool. He throws those short passes and moves the chains when they have to be moved. He's even able to yell at his older teammates when necessary.

Oh, and he's also single, Damonesque-handsome, humble, rich, and charming. He's secure enough in his manhood to admit to ESPN Magazine that he has his hair professionally high-lighted and he carries a "Europe-an handbag," a.k.a. a purse.

Veteran tight end Christian Fauria said, "Women want to be with him and men want to be him... We're not jealous of him, we just want his life. Just for one day. Everybody wants to be Tom Brady. He carries himself real well."

Mindful of his riches and success, QB 12 does his best to be one of the guys. For the past three years, he's won one of the coveted preseason parking spaces for top dedication during the offseason workouts. He's careful to credit all those around him. He steers clear of star treatment. He does not big-time his teammates.

> Brady will never have the raw skills of Manning, but he's on his way to Montana and we don't mean I-94 from North Dakota.

"Never," said Fauria. "You wouldn't get away with that in this locker room. Guys pick up on that right away. He knows that and it's not his way, so it doesn't matter."

Brady will never have the raw skills of Manning, but he's on his way to Montana and we don't mean I-94 from North Dakota. The road to Montana is paved with Super Bowl gold.

Manning outpoints Brady Sunday. More completions. More yards. More beautiful throws.

But Brady wins and goes to Super Bowl XXXVIII in Houston. ◆

The Streak

by SEAN SMITH

February 2, 2004 | As inglorious as this season began, the Patriots quickly made it one to remember in New England. Through September, there was barely a hint of greatness. As the weather cooled, though, expectations rose with the quality of play. With a 14-game winning streak in tow, Bill Belichick's squad had a chance to cement its status as one of the top teams in NFL history with a victory in Super Bowl XXXVIII. Here's a look at how the 2003 campaign took shape.

GAME 1 — 9-7-03

BUFFALO 31 | NE 0   AWAY

The curiously timed release of longtime defensive leader Lawyer Milloy triggered a few raised eyebrows, national media scrutiny, and a season-opening flogging by the Bills. Many Patriots players later admitted Milloy's sudden relocation was a major distraction, and it showed. Buffalo had scoring drives of 80 and 90 yards on its opening two possessions. Tom Brady suffocated under the Buffalo pressure, tying his career high with four interceptions and managing just 123 yards passing. As for Milloy, the safety had an interception, sack, five tackles, and an ear-to-ear grin. **Record: 0-1.**

GAME 2 — 9-14-03

NE 31 | PHILADELPHIA 10   AWAY

In the first sign of the Patriots' immeasurable tenacity, New England managed to shake off any Buffalo hangover and throttle the Eagles, forcing six turnovers, recording seven sacks, and sending a dejected Donovan McNabb to the bench with his worst outing in years (18 of 46, 186 yards, 2 interceptions, 2 lost fumbles). In a six-minute span in the second quarter, Brady (30 of 44, 255 yards, 3 TDs) connected with Christian Fauria on two scoring passes. Brady added a 26-yard touchdown toss to Deion Branch in the third quarter. Win No. 1 was about as easy they came this season. **Record: 1-1.**

GAME 3   9-21-03

NE 23 | NY JETS 16   **HOME**

It was your typical roughhouse matchup between the AFC East rivals, so physical that Ted Washington (leg), David Patten (leg), and Ty Law (ankle) all left the field. But New York was hindered by injures, too, namely quarterback Chad Pennington, who was recuperating from a dislocated wrist. That put Vinny Testaverde in charge of the Jets offense, and he threw an interception that rookie Asante Samuel used to make a name for himself, bringing it back 55 yards for a fourth-quarter touchdown. Brady broke a 9-9 tie at the end of the third quarter with his only rushing touchdown of the season, calling his own number from a yard out. An earlier sack by Sam Cowart had left a grimacing Brady holding his right elbow, but he stayed in to oversee an offense that gained 147 yards rushing and 147 yards passing. **Record: 2-1.**

GAME 4   9-28-03

WASHINGTON 20 | NE 17   **AWAY**

It's easy to forget just how close the Patriots came to starting their winning streak a week earlier. The Redskins scored 14 points in the third quarter to cultivate a 20-3 advantage, then watched a sore-armed Brady go to work. First came a 29-yard touchdown pass to David Givens on a 71-yard march in the third quarter. Then with 2:10 to play, Brady drew New England within 3, but the Patriots ran out of time. Three of New England's four turnovers came via Brady interceptions. **Record: 2-2.**

GAME 5   10-5-03

NE 38 | TENNESSEE 30   **HOME**

Unsung heroes became the driving force on a team that wouldn't lose. In his first game back from a four-game suspension for violating the league's steroid policy, former Boston College standout Mike Cloud gave the Patriots' running game a lift by providing 73 yards and two scores, including the go-ahead 15-yarder with 3:14 to go. The touchdown followed a 71-yard kickoff return by rookie Bethel Johnson. Steve McNair threw for 391 yards and ran for two scores for the Titans, but his failed rally was set back when a gimpy Law stepped in front of a pass intended for Tyrone Calico and went 65 yards the other way for a 38-27 lead with 1:49 remaining. The streak is on, and the Titans haven't seen the last of it. **Record: 3-2.**

GAME 6   10-12-03

NE 17 | NY GIANTS 6   **HOME**

Twenty-nine yards and one first down in the first half. Not for the Giants, but the Patriots, who suffered an early offensive blackout. If not for a Matt Chatham 38-yard fumble return on New York's third play from scrimmage, this would've meant serious trouble. Instead, New England held a 7-3 halftime lead. Brady, who was 7 of 11 for 105 yards in the second half, engineered a 10-play, 85-yard quest that resulted in a 17-3 lead. New York held almost every statistical advantage except on the scoreboard. Kerry Collins was picked off four times, and only two field goals were to show for the Giants' 381 total yards and 35 minutes of possession. For the Patriots, this was a harbinger of defensive supremacy at home. **Record: 4-2.**

There's cause for celebration after cornerback Ty Law's interception is returned 65 yards for a touchdown during fourth-quarter action at Gillette Stadium on Oct. 5. The Patriots defeat the Titans, 38-30, to begin an unforgettable win streak.

GAME 7

10-19-03

NE 19	MIAMI 13	OT	AWAY

A little help never hurts during a win streak, and the Dolphins sure were gracious as the Patriots broke a 13-game skid in Miami in September and October. OK, Brady had something to do with it, too. ... Miami had two prime chances to put an end to New England's modest two-game run. With Olindo Mare, the league's second-most accurate kicker, poised to connect from 35 yards with two minutes left, Richard Seymour preserved the tie with a clutch block. Mare had another chance on the Dolphins' first overtime possession, but pushed another 35-yard bid wide right. The Patriots didn't immediately capitalize, but Tyrone Poole's interception of Jay Fiedler at the New England 18 made sure the offense would get another shot. It took Brady (24 of 34, 283 yards) just one play to end it, hitting Troy Brown on a slant, and Brown outran the defense for 82 yards for the team's longest reception of the season. **Record: 5-2.**

GAME 8   10-26-03

NE 9 | CLEVELAND 3   HOME

It's tough for any opposing offense to dictate the action at Gillette Stadium. For a team with two injured quarterbacks, why bother? Turning first to Tim Couch (sprained thumb) then Kelly Holcomb (broken fibula), the Browns somehow averaged more yards per rush (4.4) than per pass (3.0), even without leading rusher William Green. The Patriots defense allowed Cleveland to cross midfield just twice. The only reason the outcome was still in doubt in the fourth quarter was because the Patriots offense kept faltering on third down (4 of 14) and in the red zone (three Adam Vinatieri field goals). A bright spot was a breakthrough game for tight end Daniel Graham, who made seven catches for 110 yards. **Record: 6-2.**

GAME 9   11-3-03

NE 30 | DENVER 26   AWAY

It could've been a long Monday night. Very long. Brady fumbled the second snap, and four plays later, Denver had a 7-0 lead. Brady's third pass was intercepted, and the Broncos had a chance for more. Then things got really interesting. Brady hit Branch for a 66-yard score, and Johnson again proved his value as a returner with a 63-yard runback. Brady's sensational second half began with a 6-yard touchdown pass to Graham for a brief lead. Brief because Deltha O'Neal gave it back to Denver three minutes later with a 57-yard punt return. After Vinatieri had brought the Patriots within 1, Belichick opted for an intentional safety with 2:49 left to hinder Denver's field position. Risky but reasonable. New England forced a punt,

and six plays later, Brady (20 of 35, 350 yards, 3 TDs) found Givens in the end zone with 30 seconds left for the winning 18-yard score. Hello to the bye week. **Record: 7-2.**

GAME 10   11-16-03

NE 12 | DALLAS 0   HOME

A three-ring circus descended on Foxborough — one for Bill Parcells's Cowboys, one for Belichick's Patriots, and one for the media frenzy surrounding this Sunday night matchup between playoff-bound teams. What everyone was treated to was New England's first shutout in the Belichick era, a truly deflating experience for Parcells since Dallas outgained the Patriots, 291 yards to 268. Quincy Carter threw three interceptions (twice picked off by Law) and Dallas averaged 3 yards per rush. Brady didn't fare much better (15 of 34, 212 yards), but he was turnover free. **Record: 8-2.**

GAME 11   11-23-03

NE 23 | HOUSTON 20 | OT   AWAY

Statistical dominance aside (and a 472-169 edge in total net yards is just that), New England needed a few great escapes to preserve its streak and improve to a franchise-best 9-2. Twice the Patriots settled for 3 points in goal-to-go situations; two of their three turnovers led to Texan touchdowns. Vinatieri plunked the right upright on a 38-yard attempt before halftime. It was up to Brady to erase a late 7-point deficit, moving the offense 80 yards in the final minutes and finding Graham in the end zone on fourth down to force overtime. New England's first shot at victory resulted in a blocked Vinatieri attempt from 35 yards. Houston didn't capitalize on a poor Ken Walter punt, and this time, with a tie looming, the Patriots moved 76 yards to put Vinatieri in position for his winning 28-yard kick with 41 seconds remaining. **Record: 9-2.**

GAME 12   11-30-03

NE 38 | INDIANAPOLIS 34   AWAY

For all the Patriots did right, so much so soon went wrong. If not for a single yard, their Super Bowl run might have taken on a different complexion. Brady was on target early, setting up a 43-yard Vinatieri field goal and a 4-yard touchdown run by Cloud. When Brady found Dedric Ward for a 31-yard scoring pass the lead was 17-0. It would grow to 31-10, then came the flurry. A Brady interception led to a Manning touchdown. Another Brady pick, another Manning score. A Patriot punt, another Manning TD, this one to tie it at 31. Brady regrouped for a 13-yard scoring strike to Branch with 8:36 remaining, and the rest was up to the New England defense. Down 4 on their final drive, the Colts reached the Patriots' 1 before Willie McGinest blasted through the pile and stuffed Edgerrin James for a 1-yard loss on fourth down. Streak is preserved at eight and counting. **Record: 10-2.**

GAME 13   12-7-03

NE 12 | MIAMI 0   HOME

No one was expecting much stylistically, not with more than 2 feet of snow turning Gillette Stadium into an oversized igloo. So how did Foxborough become a hearth of humanity? How about a second AFC East title in three years, not to mention a shutout and season sweep of a hated rival? The run-oriented weather not only failed to play into Miami's hands (Ricky Williams had just 68 yards, Matt Turk punted a team-record 11 times) it compounded a horrendous

day for Fiedler, who was sacked five times and picked off twice. His second interception was a disaster, plucked off the line of scrimmage by Tedy Bruschi and returned 5 yards to make it 10-0 with 8:55 to play. New England managed just 2.3 yards per carry and 36.5 yards per punt (they also had 11 total). Branch was on the receiving end of 93 of Brady's 163 yards passing. **Record: 11-2.**

GAME 14   12-14-03

NE 27 | JACKSONVILLE 13   HOME

For the first time in 19 quarters at Gillette Stadium, an opponent reached the end zone. Not that it mattered much. The Patriots' franchise-record 12th win of the season was already secure. Brady connected with Graham for a 27-yard score on the team's opening possession (he was 6 for 6 on the drive), and finished 22 of 34 for 228 yards. Jacksonville retaliated with two drives inside the red zone, but settled for field goals. In his first action since Nov. 3, Brown was the recipient of a 10-yard touchdown pass, good for a 20-6 lead early in the fourth quarter. Playing catch-up in the snow didn't work out for Jaguars rookie Byron Leftwich; he was picked off twice by Poole, and the second enabled Antowain Smith to tack on a 1-yard touchdown run in the fourth quarter. **Record: 12-2.**

GAME 15   12-20-03

NE 21 | NY JETS 16   AWAY

It was a quick turnaround for a Saturday night affair at the Meadowlands. Too bad for the Jets, Pennington was the one who looked like he was sleep-walking. Patriots defenders were seemingly everywhere; they intercepted Pennington five times (he had never even thrown three in one game), and sacked him on four occasions. Pennington's opening pick (by Bruschi) led to Brady's 35-yard touchdown pass to Givens on New England's first offensive play. McGinest returned his second-quarter interception 15 yards to break a 7-7 tie. New England's offensive focus was on the ground, with Smith (18 carries, 121 yards) giving the Patriots their first 100-yard rusher in 22 contests. Givens and Brady collaborated again in the third quarter for a 5-yard scoring pass. **Record: 13-2.**

GAME 16   12-27-03

NE 31 | BUFFALO 0   HOME

You know Larry Izzo was paying attention. With his team just decimating the Bills (it was 28-0 at halftime), Izzo helped keep Buffalo off the scoreboard in the waning seconds by intercepting backup Travis Brown in the end zone, providing a mirror image to the season opener. Another shutout was fitting to cap the only undefeated home season in team history. There was a laundry list of potential vindicators for the Week 1 debacle. Among them was Brady, who rebounded from his four interceptions in the first meeting to fire four touchdown passes before the break. For the third straight game, he led the Patriots to a score on their opening possession. Only the 1972 Dolphins and 1934 Bears closed out the regular season in such fashion —12 straight wins. **Record: 14-2.**

When it's cold outside, an Antowain Smith TD will fire you up, especially if it puts New England ahead 14-7 in the first half of the divisional playoff.

DIVISIONAL PLAYOFF 1-10-04

NE 17 | TENNESSEE 14   HOME

It was 4 degrees with a windchill of minus-10 at Gillette Stadium — the coldest game in Patriots history. Is New England football weather inhospitable to Southern visitors? You do the math.

On the opening drive, Brady, wearing a glove on his left hand, found Johnson in stride for 41 yards, giving the Patriots a 7-0 lead with 10:59 remaining in the quarter. It marked the fourth consecutive game in which the Patriots have scored on their first possession.

Titans QB McNair responded by quickly marching his team up field for an equalizer, and Vinatieri missed a 44-yard field goal before the Patriots went back on top after an 11-play, 57-yard drive that took advantage of a Rodney Harrison interception.

In the second half, McNair engineered a 70-yard drive to tie the game, but Brady led the Patriots to within field goal range with 4:06 remaining, and Vinatieri booted the go-ahead 46-yard field goal that Tennessee couldn't answer.

Brady's numbers weren't fancy (he threw for 201 yards and one touchdown), but the Patriots again emerged victorious because he did what he does best — logged no turnovers and executed just enough plays to help his team pull out a win. Note that before this matchup, Tennessee was the only team in the league to sack the quarterback in every regular-season game and led the league in rushing defense, yet on this day, Brady was not sacked in 41 pass attempts (21 completions). **Record: 15-2.**

AFC CHAMPIONSHIP 1-18-04

NE 24 | INDIANAPOLIS 14 HOME

How good is the Patriots defense? This time out, in light snow, they intercepted league co-MVP Manning four times — three for Law alone — and forced five turnovers. Manning came into the game with a postseason rating of 156.9 (a perfect QB rating is 158.3) and left with a rating of 35.5.

The Patriots again scored on their opening drive, marching 65 yards in 13 plays, cashing in on a 7-yard touchdown pass from Brady to Givens. Manning responded by moving the Colts to the New England 7-yard line, but was picked in the end zone by Harrison. A 31-yard Vinatieri field goal made it 10-0 early in the second, and he later upped it to 13-0 following Law's first spectacular one-handed interception. The Patriots added two on a botched-punt safety before the end of the half.

The Colts finally broke through on the first possession of the second half (15-7), but six plays and 48 yards later, the Patriots added to their lead with a 27-yard Vinatieri field goal. Vinatieri would boot two more through the uprights, giving him five total on the day (a playoff record). Meanwhile, Smith rushed for 100 yards on 22 carries, and Brady completed 22 of 37 passes (with one interception) for 237 yards and one touchdown.

Brady's predictable take on the winning streak: "To win 14 in a row, that's unbelievable. I mean, who does that? Nobody does that, and it's great will and great determination, and the preparation will lead to execution on game day by everybody. ... And still the goal really hasn't been achieved, so winning 14 in a row is great, but if there is not a 15th, then it's all for nothing." **Record: 16-2.** ♦

Exuberance is allowed on the AFC championship stage, particularly when it follows a victory over Peyton Manning's Colts. The only thing sweeter: winning a Super Bowl in Houston.

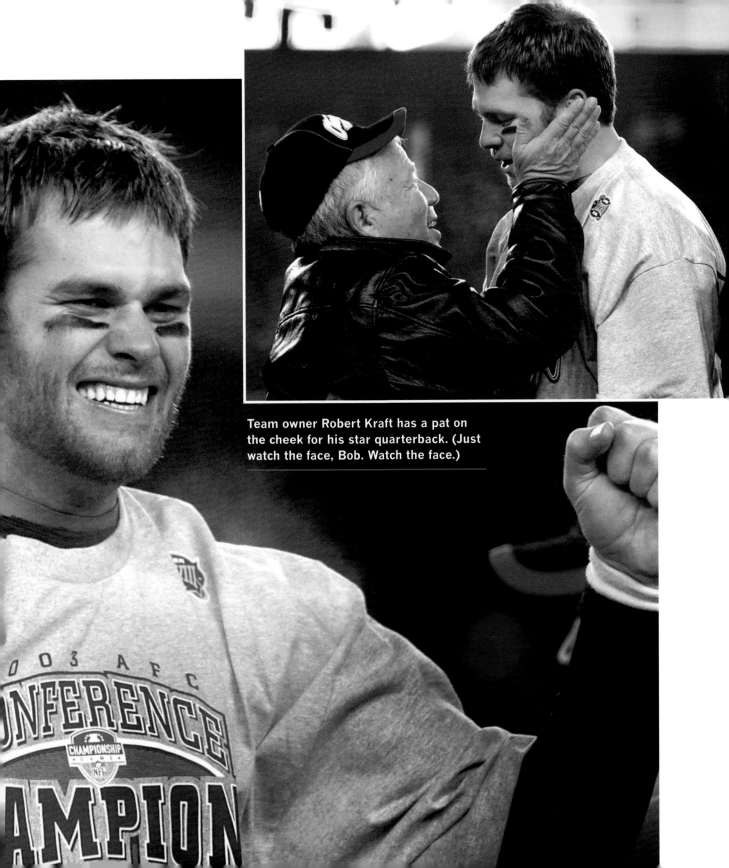

Team owner Robert Kraft has a pat on the cheek for his star quarterback. (Just watch the face, Bob. Watch the face.)

003 AFC
ONFERENCE
CHAMPIONSHIP
GAME
NFL
AMPION

SUPER BOWL XXXVIII

New Man

by JACKIE MACMULLAN

February 1, 2004 | The first time, it happened too fast. One day, Tom Brady was a young quarterback with no pro credentials who tried to meet women by telling them, "You know, I play for the Patriots . . ." It never worked. They didn't believe him, and neither did the nightclub doormen, who waved him off to the back of the line with the rest of the anonymous working stiffs. Brady would shrug, grin at his pal Dave Nugent, another no-name Patriot, and wait his turn like everyone else.

Then, suddenly, frantically, he was waved to the front of the line. Drew Bledsoe, New England's starting quarterback, suffered a sheared blood vessel in his chest against the New York Jets, and Brady was the new starter. He stepped into the job like he was slipping into an elegant, tailor-made suit. He was a perfect fit for coach Bill Belichick's offense: a cerebral, confident, natural leader.

New England won games with Brady in charge. Lots of games. Bledsoe returned, but his job was taken. Brady was careening toward stardom and the Super Bowl. Overnight he became Boston's most desirable bachelor. He was mobbed when he bought gas, so he started choosing full serve. He was overrun by fans at his old haunt, the Outback Steakhouse, so he started ordering take-out. Young girls showed up at his apartment to ask him to the prom, so he stopped answering the door.

By the time his team arrived in New Orleans to play the heavily favored St. Louis Rams in Super Bowl XXXVI, Brady was tired, overwhelmed, and frustrated. He led the Patriots to a thrilling upset, collected the MVP trophy, then, like Wade Boggs, tried to will himself invisible.

He couldn't. He didn't. He was a celebrity, stuck with all the accompanying trappings.

"All the stuff that came at me two years ago, I wasn't ready for it," Brady acknowledged. "I didn't know how to say no. I got mad at myself when I said yes. I found myself sitting at home, afraid to go out. Then, when I did go out, I felt like I was dodging bullets all day. I mean, people are following you home. How do you deal with that?"

SETTLING INTO LIFE

He is back again, ready for his second Super Bowl in three years, poised to ratchet up his celebrity to an even higher level. Yet the Brady who entertained the largest number of media of any player in Houston is no longer harried. He has learned to manage his new life as efficiently as he manages the Patriots' offense. He has come to accept the fact he can no longer just shoot out to a movie, or grab some dinner uninterrupted. He has learned to delegate his responsibilities. And he has learned to say no.

"I think I have somewhat of an idea what I'm getting into this time," Brady said. "It got so chaotic two years ago, I found myself thinking, 'When is this season going to end?' I don't feel that way this time.

"The pressure to go out and play well, the pressure to go out and win, that's there every week. I'm used to that by now."

The numbers he has submitted in critical situations are spectacular. He has a 5-0 career mark in postseason, a 7-0 record in overtime, 13 fourth-quarter comebacks in three years. He did not throw an interception at home during the regular season. If Brady leads New England to victory over the Carolina Panthers tonight, he will be the youngest quarterback to win two Super Bowls.

He is already one of the most popular. The Houston Chronicle conducted a Google search with the words "New England Patriots quarterback Tom Brady." There were 98,600 matches. The Chronicle staff then punched in "New England Patriots hunk Tom Brady." There were 119 matches. Brady is so hot, he's catapulted onto the big screen (catch him in "Stuck on You"). He is so hot the opposing quarterback, Jake Delhomme, wants to be him when he grows up, and he's three years older than Brady.

"The more he wins, the worse it will get," said Hall of Fame quarterback Joe Montana. "People love a winner. It's unfortunate, really, when you think about it, because people tend to completely forget the guys on the losing team, and many of them played pretty well.

"I do think something that needs to be looked at in general in this country is the lack of privacy people are afforded. You have people standing at the top of a hill from 800 yards away and taking a picture of you on your own front porch. Why should people be allowed to do that?"

Montana had lunch with Brady during the offseason, and shared his conversation with former Lakers star Magic Johnson about the difficulties of appearing in public.

"Magic told me this story," Montana said. "He was at an amusement park with his son, and every 5 feet he had to stop and sign an autograph. Finally, his son said, 'Hey, are you with them, or are you with me?' Magic got the message. He said after that, he decided if he was going to disappoint someone, it was going to be the strangers, not the people he loves."

"One thing I've learned in the last two years is I have to find time for myself," Brady said. "You have to do that, to keep your sanity. The other thing is you have to make sure you are able to prepare to play football. You can't let anything else get in the way of that."

GROWING RESPONSIBILITY

His teammates see a different player from two seasons ago. Brady was always composed, but now there's a sophistication that accompanies the composure.

"Tom has matured quite a bit since the last time we were here," said running back Antowain Smith. "When we were in New Orleans he was so excited he'd get in the huddle and start yelling out all the plays. I'd tell him, 'Hey, Tom, calm down. What did you just say?'"

"Tom would be in the huddle all fired up, slapping guys on the helmet," concurred offensive lineman Damien Woody. "I thought he was going to give someone a concussion."

Yet even in the middle of his first Super Bowl, Brady displayed an uncommon poise. Just 1 1/2 hours before kickoff, he curled up in front of his locker and took a nap. In the final seconds of the game, as the Patriots po-

sitioned themselves in field goal range, Brady intentionally spiked the ball to stop the clock. The ball bounced back up, and then he instinctively balanced the ball on his hand for a moment, before flicking it back.

"It's just something quarterbacks do sometimes," Brady said. "Like Tiger Woods hitting the golf balls on his driver."

But was it prudent to engage in such frivolity moments before the game would be decided?

"I don't know," the quarterback said with a shrug. "I thought we had the game pretty well in hand."

He was more naive then. Wasn't football fun? He learned differently when his close friend, Lawyer Milloy, was released days before this year's opener because the safety and the team couldn't agree on restructuring his contract. Brady was surprisingly candid in expressing disappointment in the organization for cutting his friend loose. Those comments, said Brady, led to a visit from owner Robert Kraft after New England got thumped by Milloy's new team, the Buffalo Bills.

"Robert talks to me a lot," Brady said. "He has a way of looking at things differently. He's been through a lot of tough things in his own life. He came to me and said, 'I was really worried about you after that game. You seemed so angry. You weren't yourself.' His message was he wanted me to get over it quickly. And I did. And we turned it around."

While Kraft and coach Bill Belichick probably would have preferred that Brady keep his comments to himself, the quarterback's willingness to articulate what so many of his teammates were thinking did not go unnoticed in the locker room.

"Tom is the team spokesman," Woody said. "We all understand he has to pick his spots. Tom has a lot of responsibility on his shoulders. But when it came to the Lawyer thing, he had some things to get off his chest. If

> "One thing I've learned... is I have to find time for myself."

This field general is up for battle, and he puts the Carolina Panthers on notice in Houston.

he had said anything different than what he did say, it wouldn't have been genuine."

The willingness to be outspoken comes with experience. If Brady is going to carry the load, he should have the right to speak about the weight of it.

"I never felt like I could say anything [my first year as a starter]," Brady said. "I hadn't earned it. You earn that by showing up on time, by performing consistently, by working out with the team, by putting in your time. When I see new young guys come in and start yapping, I tell them to shut up."

PRIORITIES IN LINE

If he could do something over, he would not have let his post Super Bowl commitments keep him from his annual vacation with his father. He would have shared more of his success with friends. He would have skipped some of the parties.

His time remains at a premium, but he will not let it interfere with what is truly important to him. When, for instance, offensive coordinator Charlie Weis awoke from stomach reduction surgery that initially left him comatose, the first person he saw was his wife. The second was his young quarterback, who had kept a vigil at his bedside.

"He said, 'If I didn't come, I was afraid you were going to yell at me again,'" Weis recalled. "He stayed for 48 hours. He even told my wife, 'Go. Eat. I'll wait here.'"

Brady will be there for them. His coaches and his teammates know that. If he leads the New England Patriots to another Super Bowl win, he will brace for the inevitable avalanche of opportunities, demands, and responsibili-

ties. If his team loses, he will lose a little luster. No matter. He has plenty to spare.

Late last week, a reporter asked Brady if he preferred that the dome at Reliant Stadium be open or closed for the big game. "Open or closed," Brady mused. "Why, is it my decision?"

Last time we checked, it wasn't. Too bad. That kid in front of the line has a pretty good knack for making the right decisions. ♦

New England fans are clamoring for another Lombardi Trophy.

Repeat!

by DAN SHAUGHNESSY

February 2, 2004 | Groundhog Day.

Adam Vinatieri's 41-yard field goal with four seconds remaining gave the New England Patriots a 32-29 victory over the Carolina Panthers last night in Super Bowl XXXVIII.

Yogi Berra would have called it "Deja vu all over again."

It was all so familiar... Vinatieri kicking the game-winner... quarterback Tom Brady winning the Most Valuable Player Award... coach Bill Belichick and owner Bob Kraft hoisting the Vince Lombardi Trophy while Patriot players hugged and brushed confetti off one another. All of these things happened two years ago when the Patriots upset the St. Louis Rams in New Orleans.

Kraft told the crowd last night, "Fifty-three players, 17 coaches, a head coach — the heart and soul of our team showed us what the concept of team is all about."

Championships are like children — you love each one equally. But the manner in which the 2003-04 Patriots went about their business makes this title a slightly favored son. The Patriots finished the season with 15 consecutive wins, went 10-0 against winning teams, and went 10 weeks without trailing in a game before the Panthers put them on the ropes last night at Houston's Reliant Stadium.

As ever, Brady was Joe Montana-cool under pressure. With the game tied and a little more than a minute to play, he moved the Patriots 37 yards in six plays, setting up Vinatieri's winner. The clutch kicker had missed a 31-yard chip shot, and had another attempt blocked, but his final boot was straight and true.

"Maybe a little deja vu of two years ago," said Vinatieri. "The fellows moved the ball downfield and we had the opportunity to win it again. This never gets old. With this type of venue and the pressure on, it's never easy, but you try to block all the external things out and kick it. I'll cherish this for a long time."

Meanwhile, what's left for Brady? John Kerry's running mate? First man on Mars? Starting pitcher for the Red Sox when they finally win a World Series? The 26-year-old golden child becomes the youngest two-time Super Bowl-winning quarterback and one of only four players to win the MVP Award twice. He completed 32 of 48 passes for 354 yards and three touchdowns. He is 6-0 lifetime in playoff games.

"The guys made some great catches there on that last drive," said Brady. "And Adam drove that sucker right down the middle to win it. What a game. Fitting for the Super Bowl, I guess."

When the Patriots trailed for the first time since before Thanksgiving, Brady moved them 68 yards on 11 plays and regained the lead with a 1-yard touchdown pass to linebacker Mike Vrabel. When the Panthers roared back to tie the game, Brady responded again.

"It was an awesome year," said Belichick. "I can't say enough about the players. We finished the game with two backup safeties. That's the way it's been all year."

Once again, he's the Super Bowl MVP. And boy, this never gets old.

So now it's Groundhog Day, where the scene keeps repeating itself, much like in the Bill Murray movie, but there's no one left to beat. Too bad. Patriots fans surely would embrace six more weeks of football. In the wake of the coldest January since 1888, and the most disappointing Red Sox finish since 1986, New England needed a lift, and the Patriots delivered with a season for the ages.

In the end, the Super Bowl win was like so many others in this magical Patriots season. The Patriots failed to overwhelm their opponents, relied on strong defense, got contributions from the entire roster, and left it to Brady and Vinatieri to come through at the finish. The fact that New England's final touchdown pass was caught by a linebacker tells you much of what you need to know about this team.

By any measure, these Patriots go into the books as one of the best and most beloved Boston sports teams of the last 100 years. Not since the Larry Bird Celtics of 1984 and '86 has a local team won two championships in three seasons. The Bruins last did it in 1970 and '72 and the Red Sox haven't turned the trick since 1916 and '18.

The 2003-04 Patriots featured one of the best defenses in league history, used 42 different starters, had only two Pro Bowlers, and took pride in selflessness and interchangeable parts. At times, it looked as if they had 11 coaches on the field. They transformed their two-year-old stadium into the happiest place on earth.

The camaraderie of the Patriots was evident at the start again last night. Troy Brown, the senior Patriot in continuous service, led the AFC champions onto the field. And as they did two years ago, the Patriots poured out of their tunnel en masse — a show of unity that was copied by the Panthers. It was clear at this moment that the Super Bowl would be like

> "At times it looked as if they had 11 coaches on the field."

another home game for Belichick's team. Patriot Nation made its presence felt and there were moments when Reliant Stadium sounded like the football theater off Route 1 in Foxborough.

It started out like a World Cup game and was still 0-0 with a little more than three minutes to play in the first half. But Brady threw a pair of touchdown passes in the final three minutes and Carolina's Jake Delhomme started to move his team and New England led, 14-10, at intermission.

After a ribald halftime show featuring Janet Jackson, play was interrupted briefly when a streaker managed to line up with the Panthers for the opening kickoff. He was chased by authorities and eventually brought down when Patriots linebacker Matt Chatham put a shoulder into him. Needless to say, Belichick was not amused.

It got wild again after a scoreless third quarter. The teams traded touchdowns early in the fourth. After a Brady interception, the Panthers struck again on the longest play from scrimmage in Super Bowl history, an 85-yard pass from Delhomme to Muhsin Muhammad. Carolina led, 22-21, with 6:53 left.

Brady went to work and it was madness the rest of the way. As always, the Patriots came through in the clutch.

No doubt there will be whispers of "dynasty." The well-managed, brilliantly coached Patriots are in position to make it back to the national stage in Jacksonville next year. In the meantime, there are rings on order and the Patriots will be feted in City Hall's canyon of heroes tomorrow.

"None of this would be possible without the fans back in Boston," Brady shouted from the podium. "We'll be back [tomorrow] for the parade!" ♦

Unflappable

by KEVIN PAUL DUPONT

February 2, 2004 | It wasn't as if a tattered script fell from the Reliant Stadium roof, a remnant from New Orleans two Super Bowls ago. But as the final moments played out here last night, Carolina receiver Ricky Proehl felt as if he had seen it all before, the ending playing out before his eyes once more.

"[Tom] Brady going down the field," said Proehl, who two years ago was a member of the St. Louis Rams club that was stunned by New England in the Super Bowl. "The same thing... and [Adam] Vinatieri kicked the field goal. When it was over, I had the sick feeling again."

Cool, calm, and seemingly unflappable, Brady further burnished his image as a clutch postseason performer, connecting on 32 of 48 passes, good for 354 yards and three touchdowns, and pacing the Patriots to a come-from-behind 32-29 Super Bowl victory over the defensively-tenacious Panthers.

The 26-year-old Brady, with only 68 seconds remaining in regulation, once again marched his squad downfield. Over the next 59 seconds, the Patriots chewed up 37 yards in five plays, bringing the ball to the Carolina 23. Over on the sideline, Proehl's stomach was beginning to flip.

"When we need 'em, they cash in," said Deion Branch, reflecting on whether Brady or Vinatieri was the calmest under pressure. "Both of 'em [are the same]. The coaches always say, 'When your number's called, you've got to cash in.'"

Brady further cashed in after the win when he was named the MVP, winning a Cadillac XLR. He also was named the MVP two years ago.

Branch and Brady tried to connect to open the winning drive, but the result was the last of Brady's 16 incompletions. Then came a 13-yard pass to Troy Brown, followed by another to Brown for 20 more, which was nullified for offensive pass interference. Brown redeemed himself with a 13-yard catch on the next snap. The next two plays had Brady first hitting Daniel Graham for 4 more yards, and then a 17-yard hookup with Branch. The ball was at the Carolina 23, and Vinatieri was on his way in from the sideline.

"I was just trying to get it a little closer there to shorten the field goal," said Branch. "They had a short coverage there, because they figured out what we were doing. My thought there is, if I can score, I try to score, but I just want to get as close for Adam as I can."

Brady, his helmet off, watched from the sideline as Vinatieri ripped through the ball with his right foot. It couldn't have been more than 10 feet into flight when Vinatieri, who earlier missed a chip shot and had another attempt blocked, raised a clenched right fist. He knew where it was going, and he knew the Patriots

Football's biggest rush is celebrating a Super Bowl victory. Brady and his Patriots know the feeling, again, after drowning the Panthers 32-29.

were going home winners.

"Adam drilled it right down the middle to win it," said a beaming Brady, sounding more California mellow than East Coast jubilant at the postgame podium. "What a game. What a game. Fitting for a Super Bowl, I guess."

The Patriots had not trailed since last being in Houston Nov. 23. But neither Brady nor

anyone else on the New England sideline so much as flinched under the pressure.

"We've been down before," he said. "We just don't lose composure."

If not for the winning drive, Brady risked his signature moment of the night being his pass, intended for Christian Fauria with 7:48 left in the fourth, that Reggie Howard picked off

Left: Wide receiver Deion Branch is on the receiving end of both a touchdown pass and a bear hug from his quarterback as they celebrate putting New England up 7-0 on the way to more Super Bowl glory.

Below: The red, white and blue team wins a spiffy new banner to hang at Gillette Stadium. Right beside the one they have from 2001, and the one they'll get for 2004.

in the end zone and ran back to the 10. Four plays later, Jake Delhomme threw an 85-yard touchdown pass to Muhsin Muhammad, ultimately lifting the Panthers to the 22-21 lead.

Flustered? Who, Brady?

"That's what happens in the Super Bowl, you know?" said Brady. "They make great plays, too."

There is a confidence in the Patriots, said Brady, in which they believe they can "win anything." "But to win this, the way we did it," he added. It's just unbelievable the way we did it."

Making it all the more remarkable, he said, was that his offensive line kept him from getting sacked across the full 60 minutes.

"And that," he said, crediting the ferocious

Carolina defense, "is the most heat I've had all year."

Brady began to run the numbers, as if still rolling through the playbook.

"A 60-minute game, to come down to the last 5 seconds?" he said. "It think it tells you about the optimism of the two teams."

Two Super Bowls. A pair of victories. Matching MVPs. The inevitable comparisons to former 49ers great Joe Montana.

"I said all week, he's the benchmark for quarterbacks in the league," said Brady, gingerly sidestepping undesired pressure one last time. "This is only my fourth year, and in no way am I close to that. Hopefully, one day I'm on that level, but not yet." ◆

Already Legend

by DAN SHAUGHNESSY

February 3, 2004 | Get out the chisels and sand blasters. Time to put Tom Brady's handsome face on Boston's professional sports Mt. Rushmore Monument.

This is no small honor. Only four men have had their faces carved into the side of our imaginary mountain — Ted Williams, Bill Russell, Bobby Orr, and Larry Bird. Four seemed like the right number when Bird went up and we thought his big beak might be the last nose sculpted on the side of Mt. Fame.

Now Brady. He belongs.

This will strike some as sacrilegious. After all, Brady has been a Patriot for only four years and one of those seasons was spent on the bench. So how can a guy with three full seasons join the likes of Teddy Ballgame, Russ, Bobby, and Larry?

Simple. Championships and Super Bowl MVP performances enable Brady to pass Yaz, Pedro, Rocket, Milt, Hondo, Hannah, Nomar, Bourque, Cooz, and the other gods of our games.

Fresh off this latest, surreal Super Bowl win, Brady was working on one hour of sleep when he walked to the second floor ballroom podium in Houston's Hilton Americas Hotel at 8:30 a.m. yesterday. He accepted the MVP award with his usual graciousness, crediting teammates and charming the national media with his humor, good manners, and a Chiclets smile. He is the John F. Kennedy of professional sports. (Does that make Foxborough Camelot?) Make no mistake about it, people; Brady has gone national and he has spilled into pop culture. He's gone from NESN to ESPN to "Entertainment Tonight." From the Boston Globe to Sports Illustrated to People. His appearance at the State of the Union is only the beginning. Book deals, film roles, and sightings with royalty can't be far behind.

We know Brady isn't as talented as Ted, Russ, Bobby, or Larry. Williams, though championship-starved, was the greatest hitter who ever lived and the single biggest sports newsmaker New England ever has known. Russell changed basketball and won 11 championships in 13 years. Orr was arguably the greatest hockey player of them all and won two championships. Bird won three championships and is forever the brightest

Tom Brady's sculpted features were born ready for our imaginary stone monument to greatness.

star in the Celtic galaxy.

Now Brady. In three years he has delivered two Lombardi trophies. He is only the fourth player in NFL history to win two Super Bowl MVPs and the other three are Bart Starr, Terry Bradshaw, and Joe Montana. Brady did it earlier than any of them.

He is 40-12 lifetime as a starting QB, never has lost in overtime, and is 6-0 in the postseason. Sunday he completed more passes (32 of 48, 354 yards) than any quarterback in Super Bowl history. Twice in three years he has directed winning drives with just over a minute left on the clock. The comparisons with Montana no longer are frivolous.

If we're talking raw skills, Brady never could make it to the side of Mt. Fame. He's a sixth-round draft pick who didn't play much in college, can't run very fast, and has only an average arm.

> He's a sixth-round draft pick who didn't play much in college, can't run very fast, and has an average arm.

This hardly compares with the God-given gifts bestowed on Messrs. Williams, Russell, Orr, and Bird. But Brady earns admission on clutch play, championship delivery, and a checklist of intangibles that make him the perfect QB for a guy who's turned out to be a perfect football coach.

In no particular order, Brady is articulate, calm under pressure, tough, polite, humble, hard working, and terrific with the media. His teammates genuinely like him.

His acceptance speech yesterday morning was typical Brady.

"I've said this before about the guys in our locker room," he started. "We like playing football and we enjoy being around each other and working hard. The commitment to go out there and win. That's what's exciting. Last night when you can hug those guys and watching Rodney Harrison, who broke his arm — I mean you're trying to win for Rodney, for Mike Vrabel who three years ago was hardly playing. That's what it's really about."

Vintage Brady. Talking about teammates. Sharing the gold.

He introduced some humor when asked about Janet Jackson's halftime exhibition (commissioner Paul Tagliabue sounded pretty hot about the "wardrobe malfunction" incident and you can expect Paul Anka, Pat Boone, and the Osmonds next year in Jacksonville, Fla.). "I heard about it," said Brady.

He paused.

"Wish I had seen it. Maybe I'll get it on the replay."

So what's left for Brady after today's parade? He's only 26.

"As great at it was, it wasn't perfect," he started. "There's always things to improve on. I just enjoy playing football.

"I like going out there and I like lifting weights and I like the offseason stuff and I like the training camps. I do. I like practice. And hopefully I'll just keep doing that for a long time.

"When I was at Michigan, we used to ask our equipment manager - he'd been there like 40 years and had a lot of rings - and we'd say, 'Hey, what's your favorite ring?' And he'd say, 'The next one.'" ♦

Top right: Like a god from on high, Brady leans to embrace teammate Rodney Harrison in the wake of the Patriots' victory over the Carolina Panthers in Super Bowl XXXVIII at Houston's Reliant Stadium.

Bottom right: The Lombardi Trophy is again in the hands of Patriots, thanks to their two-time Super Bowl MVP.

2004 SEASON

Been There

by JACKIE MACMULLAN

April 2, 2004 | Poof. Now you see him, now you don't. **Tom Brady, Super Bowl MVP and legend in the making, beat Carolina for his second championship ring in three years, made a return trip to Disney World, underwent secret shoulder surgery, appeared as a spectator at a celebrity outing, then disappeared.**

We haven't seen him since. Our last public image of Boston's hottest sports figure was Brady and his injured wing walking along the fairways at Pebble Beach, engulfed by his adoring public.

"I saw that on TV," reports Damien Woody, Brady's former teammate. "It was a scene. I was thinking, 'What is he doing out there? The guy is nuts.'"

Poof. The guy was also gone. Unlike after his first Super Bowl triumph, when Brady dropped in at the Playboy Mansion, scored a cameo appearance at the Oscars, and danced the night away at some of America's hottest nightclubs, this time he celebrated in private. He spent three weeks overseas with his girlfriend, Bridget Moynihan, and eschewed most late-night revelry. Inquiring minds wondered about the arthroscopic procedure on his shoulder, which team officials kept reminding us was minor, but nervous Patriots fans knew any kind of operation on this golden throwing arm shouldn't be characterized as trivial.

No, not prom night (though it is June). Brady and his lady, model/actress Bridget Moynahan, arrive at the Massachusetts home of team owner Robert Kraft, where Super Bowl XXXVIII championship rings are handed out.

Your worries are over. Brady has participated in the team's offseason conditioning program for the past three days down in Foxborough, and his agent, Don Yee, reports Brady is pain-free and ready to go.

"He's been doing everything," concurs Patriots owner Robert Kraft.

In the meantime, those endorsement offers keep on coming, along with subtle pressure from the NFL to fulfill a role as its charismatic poster boy. Brady has politely declined invites to beauty pageants, a starring role in a TV reality series, all the late-night shows, and dozens of endorsement enticements.

"That's great," says Kraft. "He's kept a very low profile. The first time, he was like a little kid, an innocent child, reacting to everything that came at him. This time, having been through the process, he's much more prepared. He's managing his life this time, instead of other people managing his life."

Woody says flying below the radar is fine, but it makes it hard to track down his friend. He's been trying to reach Brady for weeks.

"I can't get him," Woody moans. "We keep missing each other. I call him up — nothing. He calls me back — nothing. I haven't talked to him since I signed my deal [with Detroit], so I'll call him again this week. I want to know how he's doing with that surgery."

Brady's shoulder woes were kept quiet during the season, per order of coach Bill Belichick. Woody says the injury was, at times, debilitating.

"A lot of people didn't see the inside story of last season," Woody claims. "Tom was in a lot of pain. People have no idea what he went through to play. He was in the training room all the time getting treatment. I'm telling you, that guy is tough."

Woody said what he'll miss most about Brady is his ability to maintain a healthy relationship with his teammates as his popularity soars.

"He's one of the guys," Woody explains. "Sometimes you meet quarterbacks who isolate themselves from the rest of the team. Tom never did that.

"I'm not surprised he hasn't done much [in the offseason]. I think he's feeling a little bit of been there, done that. He's just collecting his rings and going about his business. I definitely don't want to downplay a Super Bowl victory, and of course everyone was

> # "He's managing his life this time, instead of other people managing his life."

celebrating and happy when we won the second one. But it wasn't like the first. Guys went to the parade, then went their own way. They weren't showing up on TV every five minutes like after the first one."

Brady will reemerge in the public eye over the next several weeks, particularly for some charitable endeavors he supports. Yee said his client's popularity remains staggering, and they are still finding their way when it comes to what should and shouldn't be done. The agent and the QB view this career as a long-term project that has only just begun.

"The word I would use is nascent," Yee explains. "Tom has two skins on the wall, but he'd like more. There are still other things to accomplish."

One of Brady's laments after the first Super Bowl win was he became so overwhelmed with invitations, he failed to carve out time for his annual golf trip with his dad, Tom Sr.

"We'll be getting it in this year," reports the proud father. "Tommy will also be with us for a family vacation in July.

"I think he's enjoyed [the Super Bowl post Season] more this time. He knows how to control the process. He has no interest in being a celebrity, but he knows he is one. He just makes sure it doesn't get in the way of his life."

Brady has done some light throwing but, according to his father, will take his time returning to form. He has easily handled all the conditioning drills this week, but as soon as they are over, poof. He's gone.

This time around, good luck finding him. ♦

Done That

by JOE BURRIS

September 9, 2004 | Remember this amazing run of Patriots prominence. In decades to come, those who rewrite sports history are bound to tell the story with such poetic license that the record will have to be set straight.

When Tom Brady's feats are summed up for posterity, allow for some creative prose and overstatement. But remind those who will listen that above all, the star quarterback had a knack for winning — not for heroics, not for drama, not for thrills.

Some may point to Brady's performance in Super Bowl XXXVI — when he led a drive with 1:51 left that set up kicker Adam Vinatieri's winning 48-yard field goal — or last season's 82-yard pass to Troy Brown in overtime to defeat Miami. Works of art? Testaments of courage? No, more like the right plays with the right precision at the right time.

The great thing about Brady is you can't easily categorize or stereotype him. He's neither blue-collar nor flashy, neither demonstrative nor unassuming. He's not fast. He's not slow. For many of the wins in which he led the Patriots, what you remember most is that the Patriots won.

He has great physical, emotional, and mental aptitude, a command for his craft and unquenchable confidence. But Brady never will be confused with Sonny Jurgensen or Sonny Liston, Bert Jones or Smarty Jones. He simply does his job better than most QBs.

Brady is success in its purest form. He does whatever it takes to win, and perhaps someday his exploits may lead some to rethink how quarterbacks are judged. Critics may say Dan Marino had a better release, Fran Tarkenton was better on the run, Roger Staubach threw a tighter spiral. But Brady has the most completions in a Super Bowl game (32 in Super Bowl XXXVIII) and of the five Super Bowl quarterbacks who completed at least 28 passes (Jim Kelly in Super Bowls XXVII and XXVI, Marino in Super Bowl XIX, Neil O'Donnell in Super Bowl XXX, and Kurt Warner in Super Bowl XXXVI), only Brady led his team to victory.

What's more:

- Brady is the first quarterback in NFL history to start and win two Super Bowls before his 27th birthday. He led the Patriots to victory in Super Bowl XXXVI when he was 24 and to a win in Super Bowl XXXVIII when he was 26.

- Brady enters this season as the NFL's all-time leader in overtime wins without a defeat (7-0). Terry Bradshaw is the only other quarterback to go undefeated in at least five overtime games (5-0).

- Brady has led the Patriots to victory in 34 of 46 regular-season starts for a .739 winning percentage — the best record among any quarterback in the NFL with at least 25 starts.

- Brady threw the first 162 passes of his career without an interception. It was the longest streak to start a career in NFL history and ranks as the third-most attempts without an interception in Patriots history.

The more people liken success to superhuman athleticism, the more you see success stories such as Brady's — those who embody commitment, enthusiasm, and desire.

"Over the course of the year, you develop some things you're really good at and then you go to those things more often," said Brady. "Then, the things you're not so good at, you decide, 'These things aren't working this year.' Some teams may scheme you up differently and take away some things that are not work-

> "If you throw the ball to a more open space, there is more margin of error than if you throw the ball into a tight space."

ing well, and you try different things. I think I've gained tons of valuable experience that you can only get by playing.

"There are certain situations you're in and you learn to adjust mentally and physically. You get these two-minute drills where you don't think you make the best decisions, and sometimes [you throw] the ball away in certain situations. All the decisions you make in critical times you put them away in your memory bank. And boy, if it ever comes up again, you know how to react."

KEY QUALITIES

Patriots coach Bill Belichick, who made Brady a starter during the 2001 season, said that when you're listing the attributes of a successful NFL quarterback, you must begin with production. "The second thing is accuracy," he said. "The third thing would be a combination of intelligence, game management, and decision-making. It could be separated, but it all kind of comes back to the same thing, the game from the neck up. You can be good in two of those areas, and not good in the third, and you're not going to have much. At some point, for a good NFL quarterback, those are going to have to be above average for the guy to be successful."

The coach said he has seen vast improvement in those areas from Brady since the quarterback came to New England in 2000. "I think Tom's throwing mechanics have improved significantly since 2000... they have continued to improve even from the 2001 season," Belichick said.

Indeed, Brady is entering just his fourth season as a starter, but he is the Patriots' all-time leader in passing percentage (61.9 percent) and passer rating (85.9). Already he

By this point, he's looking pretty comfortable in practices at Gillette Stadium.

has orchestrated 15 winning drives to break the tie or take the lead in the fourth quarter or overtime.

Four of those came in postseason — though he has just six postseason appearances.

"I think he has good accuracy, and a lot of that good accuracy is combined with good decision-making, where if you throw the ball to a more open space, there is more margin of error than if you throw the ball into a tight space," Belichick added. "I think his accuracy has improved. I think it was OK as a rookie."

Brady said that at the end of each year he evaluates his progress.

"Each year in the league, I think guys tend to feel that they've experienced more and they're able to handle more things," he said. "It almost feels more second nature now than it ever did before. You put the pads on and the helmet on and you're like, 'Oh, this feels kind of normal,' whereas in the first year in the league, you're getting used to the routine, getting used to the game planning, the way plays are called, the way plays are changed, the styles of practicing, everything.

"Now, there is more of a sense of me knowing what to expect, and I think with that you have higher expectations of yourself, and the things you try to take on that continue to challenge yourself, and that's what keeps you mentally stimulated."

WINNING TRAITS

Dan Doyle, founder and executive director of the Institute of International Sport, said there are similar characteristics in athletes and coaches in all sports who have a knack for winning.

"A winner has that Paul Silas, Bill Russell, Hondo [John] Havlicek ability to be fero-

ciously competitive yet in full control, particularly at critical junctures of the game," Doyle said. "During competition, winners employ the sports psychology mantra of staying in the present, they don't worry about what just happened or what will happen.

"Winners have the important ability to put disappointment in the past quickly. We found that winners do not dwell on failure. Rather, they view failure as a setback and learn from it."

Doyle added that Joe Montana and Bill Walsh were among many winners who spoke about the serenity of playing in the last 4-5 minutes. He said many view that time in the game as their "reward" for the work they've put in to reach a competitive level.

Brady said he's never given his accomplishments much consideration. "I think [winners are] competitive, and I think competitors don't mind any situation they're in," he said. "I'd much rather be up by 50 points at the end of the game and kneel on the ball, to tell the truth. It's not something I'm conscious of. I just go out and play like I'm capable. I just try to rally the troops."

Brady said that in the three short seasons he's been the starter, he's learned to gauge his temperament. Behind the scenes, he's constantly working to get himself "geeked up" for a game.

> "This year, I'm trying to geek myself up for that opening game... everything I'm doing now is preparation for that."

"There are certain ways you know how to prepare," said Brady. "I remember last year going into the regular season, I wasn't feeling great. And I thought I was, but evaluating, looking back on last year, I just wish I had been in a better place.

"This year, I'm trying to geek myself up for that opening game, which means everything I'm doing now is preparation for that."

The Patriots were far from sharp in the exhibition season, and Brady has said the team should not necessarily be expected to open up with Super Bowl effectiveness.

"It's a new team, it's new challenges, and everything changes," said Brady. "As much as you would like to continue on from year to year, it doesn't happen. I remember that practice before the Super Bowl and we were practicing so good, we were so crisp, we were so sharp. The receivers were doing a great job, the line was communicating great.

"Everyone knew what to expect. We went into the game and had a great game. Then you want to come out there and pick up where you left off, but it's all different. The scheme is different. The players are different. And if there's one or two new guys in there, there are a lot of things that are adjusted." ◆

Offensive lineman Stephen Neal and tight end Daniel Graham get a pile of love from their leader following Graham's touchdown catch, as New England rolls by Arizona 23-12.

Did It Again

by SEAN SMITH

February 7, 2005 | Pressure is only an illusion. To feel it you have to believe it, accept it. Pressure doesn't exist if you're a New England Patriot. It's simply not allowed.

How else do you explain a team that accomplished more in a year than most NFL teams hope to accomplish in a half-century? You say win streak, they say "What streak?" You speak of dynasty, they speak of the Carringtons. They conquer opponent after opponent with class and mash, the reflection of a coach with more mantras than a Hindu wiseman. Football is discipline, pressure is not.

These Patriots are indeed human. It's the Super Bowls, record winning streaks, and home invincibility that make them appear superhuman. Carrying the weight of history through the regular season could have slowed them down. It didn't.

GAME 1   9-9-04

NE 27 | INDIANAPOLIS 24   HOME

Indianapolis was the same offensive force it was the previous January, albeit hungrier after being dispatched from Foxborough in the AFC title game. This time, without the cold and swirling snow, it bulled its way to 446 total yards, more than enough in most weeks. Trailing, 17-13, at the half, Tom Brady (335 yards passing) sparked the New England offense with two third-quarter touchdown passes. Peyton Manning was sacked with the Colts driving for a potential tying field goal, and Mike Vanderjagt, who hadn't missed in 42 straight attempts, was forced to try a 48-yarder with 24 seconds left. The kick was wide right. Most people considered it New England's 16th straight win, but all the Patriots saw was **1-0.**

GAME 2   9-19-04

NE 23 | ARIZONA 12   AWAY

Without Corey Dillon, the Patriots' win streak may have never made it out of Tempe. The veteran running back, acquired in the offseason for a second-round draft pick, carried 32 times for 158 yards as New England held the ball for 35:16 and racked up 24 first downs. Brady supplied an early 14-0 lead with two touchdown passes to Daniel Graham before Adam Vinatieri three times bailed out the stalled offense with field goals. Arizona's offense clearly was overmatched (167 total yards), especially QB Josh McCown, who was sacked five times.

The first of the Patriots' significant injuries in 2004 came on the final play of the first half when receiver Deion Branch hurt his knee. Branch didn't return until Week 11, but his absence did benefit David Givens, who emerged as Brady's go-to receiver. **Record: 2-0.**

GAME 3   10-3-04

NE 31 | BUFFALO 17   AWAY

Tying a longstanding NFL record never felt less satisfying. The Patriots' 18th consecutive win wasn't secured until Tedy Bruschi caused a bootlegging Drew Bledsoe to fumble and Richard Seymour coasted 68 yards for the clinching score with 2:44 remaining. Many expected more against the winless Bills, with the Patriots coming off an early bye week. New England moved 77 yards on its opening possession for a 7-0 lead (Dillon 15-yard TD run), and following Vinatieri's 42-yard field goal for a 10-3 lead, Buffalo's Terrence McGee exposed one of the few Patriot flaws of 2004 by returning the ensuing kickoff 98 yards to tie the game. After Brady and Bledsoe traded scoring passes before the half, the Bills had the momentum when they forced the Patriots to settle for another Vinatieri field goal early in the fourth, but a defensive offside penalty gave New England a new set of downs, and Brady finished off a 12-play, 80-yard drive with a 2-yard touchdown pass to Graham. **Record: 3-0.**

GAME 4   10-10-04

NE 24 | MIAMI 10   HOME

Brady was intercepted on his second pass of the game, an ominous beginning to what became the quarterback's worst start of his career — 7 of 19, 76 yards, 62.6 rating. But he salvaged the day with an early 1-yard TD pass to Graham and a 5-yarder to Givens just before the half. The defense took care of the rest, battering quarterbacks Jay Fiedler (bruised ribs) and A.J. Feeley (concussion). When it was over, the team was feted for its record 19th straight win and took a minute to bask in the limelight. But only a minute. The players wondered, what's the big deal about being undefeated in October? **Record: 4-0.**

GAME 5   10-17-04

NE 30 | SEATTLE 20   HOME

Those who touted this one as a potential Super Bowl matchup were at least half right. There was no reason to doubt Seattle's legitimacy to the NFC throne, despite the fact it had blown a fourth-quarter lead to St. Louis the previous week. The Seahawks were ready for a statement game; unfortunately, that statement was "we're not ready." Matt Hasselbeck threw interceptions to end Seattle's first two series (the second gave Ty Law a franchise record-tying 36), and the Patriots turned them into a 10-0 lead. The advantage swelled to 17-0 in the second when Brady hit David Patten from 6 yards out. Brady opened the fourth quarter with consecutive turnovers, enabling the Seahawks to close within 20-17. The quarterback certainly made amends, though. On the following possession, Brady threw for 61 of the drive's 68 yards to set up another Vinatieri field goal. After Seattle tacked on

3 more, Brady found Bethel Johnson for the play of the day, a 48-yard rocket on third and 7 that paved the way for Dillon's clinching 9-yard TD run. **Record: 5-0.**

GAME 6   10-24-04

NE 13 | NY JETS 7   HOME

So few points, so much accomplished. How about an NFL-record 18 straight regular-season wins, 21 straight overall, and the first 6-0 start in franchise history? All while handing their AFC East rival its first defeat. On an overcast, drizzly afternoon, all the scoring came early. A couple of lengthy Patriot drives led to two Vinatieri field goals, and the Jets pulled ahead, 7-6, when quarterback Chad Pennington sneaked in from the 1 with two minutes left in the half. That was just enough time for New England to change the game. Johnson returned the kickoff 27 yards to the Patriots' 38. Brady hit Kevin Faulk for 24 and 5 yards, Patten for 11, and a roughing the passer penalty set up the offense at the Jets 7. Two plays later, Brady and Patten clicked again to make it 13-7 only five seconds before the break. It was a two-minute masterpiece. **Record: 6-0.**

GAME 7   10-31-04

PITTSBURGH 34 | NE 20   AWAY

For the 15th consecutive game, the Patriots scored first. That was the good news. Bad news subsequently came from all over the field. Law injured his foot midway through the opening quarter, and on the next play his replacement, Randall Gay, was burned for a 47-yard touchdown pass. Before the quarter was over, Pittsburgh piled on two more touchdowns off Brady turnovers. Without Dillon to lean on (he missed one game because of a thigh injury), Brady was overwhelmed. He fumbled away the first snap of the second half, and Jerome Bettis made it 31-10. Losses were uncharacteristic enough, but the manner of this one was shocking. The Patriots ran for just 5 yards and held the ball for a measly 17:02. Bill Belichick and his coaching staff accepted the blame, all the while making a mental list of mistakes to avoid should the teams clash again. Streak over. **Record: 6-1.**

GAME 8   11-7-04

NE 40 | ST. LOUIS 22   AWAY

Pundits predicted the pass-happy Rams would exploit a patchwork Patriots secondary, and perhaps they would have if they had the ball more often. With Dillon pounding his way to 112 yards and a touchdown, New England averaged 4.6 yards per carry and controlled the clock. St. Louis couldn't solve the blitz, leading to five Marc Bulger sacks and many poorly timed throws. Vinatieri boomed four field goals and added the first touchdown pass of his career, a 4-yarder to Troy Brown on a perfectly executed fake. Brady (234 yards) threw for multiple TDs for the sixth time in eight games, including a 2-yard toss to linebacker Mike Vrabel. Givens reached 100 yards receiving for the third straight game. A delighted Belichick called it "probably as complete a victory as I've ever been around." **Record: 7-1.**

GAME 9   11-14-04

NE 29 | BUFFALO 6   HOME

The margin of victory in this one could have been double. Seriously. New England produced points on four of its first five possessions (two Brady touchdown passes and two Vinatieri field goals) to race to a 20-0 lead. The final three quarters resembled a varsity-JV scrimmage — the Patriots had 20 first downs to Buffalo's three and had more than triple the Bills' time of possession. Buffalo's only points came on busted punt return coverage. Hard to believe these teams closed out the regular season with identical 6-1 runs. **Record: 8-1.**

GAME 10   11-22-04

NE 27 | KANSAS CITY 19   AWAY

Unlike St. Louis, the Chiefs planned to throw on the Patriots every chance they could. And they almost did, Trent Green passing 42 times for 381 yards and two scores. But with Branch (six catches, 105 yards) back in the lineup for the Monday night encounter, Brady kept pace through the air with 315 yards. His 26-yard scoring pass to Branch gave New England a 24-13 third-quarter lead, and came one play after he hit a streaking Patten for 46 yards. Dillon came up 2 yards short of his fifth straight 100-yard game. Green responded with a long TD pass to get within 24-19, but Dillon helped sustain a clinching, clock-killing drive, capped by Vinatieri's 28-yard field goal. **Record: 9-1.**

GAME 11   11-28-04

NE 24 | BALTIMORE 3   HOME

A steady downpour turned the Gillette sur-face into a quirky quagmire, neither team able to find sufficient footing or offensive consistency. And after the Patriots mis-handled their final possession of the first half, the Ravens kicked a gift field goal to enter the break tied at 3. But just when disaster knocked, New England closed the door on Baltimore. Brady drove the offense to two more field goals, then Dillon opened the fourth with a 1-yard scoring run — his 123 yards rushing were 1 fewer than Baltimore's offensive output — and the Pa-triots put it away on the next play when Ra-vens quarterback Kyle Boller was sacked by Bruschi and the ball squirted into the end zone, where it was recovered by Jarvis Green. **Record: 10-1.**

GAME 12   12-5-04

NE 42 | CLEVELAND 15   AWAY

Even by Browns standards, this one was ugly. They needed just 14 seconds to fall behind, and only three quarters to com-pletely fall apart. Johnson returned the opening kickoff 93 yards to set the rout in motion. Dillon had a field day with 100 yards on just 18 carries; he had his sec-ond touchdown before the half, and joined Brady (44-yard TD pass to Patten) on the bench in the third quarter. Brown and Rod-ney Harrison contributed interceptions, and Gay added a 41-yard fumble return. Nearly half of Cleveland's 287 total yards came in the final 15 minutes before a half-empty Dawg Pound, the pounding was that bad. **Record: 11-1.**

GAME 13   12-12-04

NE 35 | CINCINNATI 28   HOME

The Patriots already had sewn up the di-vision thanks to a Jets loss earlier in the day. Good thing, because Cincinnati piled up a Colts-like 478 total yards and 26 first downs. New England scored first for an NFL-record 18th straight game, then found it needed all the offense it could generate in the unexpected shootout. Brady's sec-ond TD pass, a 17-yarder to Christian Fau-ria midway through the third for a 35-14 spread, didn't seem so crucial at the time. But Jon Kitna kept the Cincinnati offense moving, firing a 27-yard TD pass to pull within 7 with 3:50 to go. The Bengals sim-ply ran out of time. **Record: 12-1.**

GAME 14   12-20-04

MIAMI 29 | NE 28   AWAY

The only people who gave the 2-11 Dol-phins a chance were on the sidelines. Both sidelines. The Patriots knew they would be in for a fight in one of their most haunted venues. Still, nothing seemed amiss that Monday night when Brady hit Faulk for a 31-yard touchdown on New England's open-ing possession. And even after Wes Welker's 71-yard punt return set up the tying score, there was no reason to suspect a monu-mental Miami upset. Dillon scored via the air and ground, and once Graham hauled in Brady's third TD pass, a 2-yarder with 3:59 to play, it was time to turn out the lights at 28-17. But Miami took just 1:52 to cover 68 yards (aided by a pass interference call) and Sammy Morris's 1-yard run made it a 5-point game. Instead of an onside kick, Miami opted to kick deep, and three plays later Brady served up a head-scratcher, loft-ing an easily intercepted pass into traffic.

The Patriots' secondary never looked so vulnerable as on the go-ahead score. Home-field advantage in the playoffs was history. **Record: 12-2.**

GAME 15   12-26-04

NE 23 | NY JETS 7   AWAY

Nobody felt worse about the Miami fiasco than Brady, who spent the week accepting more than his fair share of the blame. As is his trademark, though, the quarterback shook off the malaise like a half-hearted blitzer and was almost flawless as his team secured a first-round bye. Brady was 21 of 32 for 264 yards and directed five scoring drives. Dillon set the team's season rushing record. The offense sliced through a tough Jets defense with precision and surprising ease for 372 total yards and almost a 12-minute advantage in possession. The one dark cloud over New England was the third-quarter knee injury suffered by Seymour. It sure looked serious, and it turns out it was. **Record: 13-2.**

GAME 16   1-2-05

NE 21 | SAN FRANCISCO 7   HOME

This wasn't how the Patriots wanted to enter the playoffs. As much as the founding 49ers wanted their nightmare season to end, they refused to roll over. The Patriots wouldn't let them, either. Johnson's punt return for a score was negated by an illegal block, Dillon fumbled after a midfield reception, Brady threw an interception — and that was all in the first quarter. Then Dillon (116 yards rushing) and Brady conspired for a 71-yard scoring drive, with Vrabel's 1-yard catch tying the game at 7. The deadlock finally was broken midway through the third as Brady connected with Branch for an 8-yard TD, and Dillon made it 21-7 with 14:24 to play. A second consecutive 14-2 season was safe, but don't think anyone was content. "We're going to have to play a lot better than what we played today to win games in the playoffs," Vrabel said. **Record: 14-2.**

DIVISIONAL PLAYOFF   1-16-05

NE 20 | INDIANAPOLIS 3   HOME

These weren't the 49ers. The Indianapolis reserves weren't even the 49ers. This was one of the most destructive offensive forces the league has known, and with Manning as masterful as ever, it was going to take more than freezing temperatures to cool him down.

Even without Law and Seymour, the Patriots did the unthinkable, holding Indianapolis to a mere field goal and Manning to just 238 yards (a good chunk of them coming in garbage time). Edgerrin James, a big factor in the season opener, never found his groove and finished with 39 yards rushing. It was that kind of day for the Colts.

With Dillon carving out 144 yards on the ground, New England refused to relinquish possession. There was a 16-play, 9:07 drive for a field goal, a 15-play, 8:16 march for a touchdown (Brady to Givens), and a 14-play, 7:24 venture that Brady finished with a 1-yard dive for a 20-3 advantage. Quite simply, the Colts couldn't score if they didn't have the ball, and New England played an exquisite game of keepaway in winning a mind-boggling 20th straight home game.

"It was just the best game plan that we've had since I've been here," said Harrison. For a week at least. **Record: 15-2.**

AFC CHAMPIONSHIP 1-23-05

NE 41 | PITTSBURGH 27   AWAY

Belichick and his staff didn't need a week to prep for this one. The game plan wrote itself back on Halloween. You might see the same mistakes, but not from his team.

This time, the Patriots were the instant aggressors. Once-unbeatable rookie Ben Roethlisberger was intercepted on his first pass attempt, leading to Vinatieri's 48-yard kick through a stiff wind. Bettis fumbled and Brady pounced, finding Branch behind the secondary for a 60-yard score that deflated a record crowd at Heinz Field before the first quarter was over. Leading, 10-3, New England refused to let up. Brady and Branch hooked up for a 45-yard pass, which preceded a 9-yard scoring screen to a wide-open Givens. Pittsburgh showed some life by driving into Patriots' territory before Roethlisberger underthrew his target and Harrison happily took the pass 87 yards the other way to make it 24-3 at the half. Dillon and Branch, both of whom missed the October loss, combined for three touchdowns and 231 of the Patriots' 322 total yards. Indeed, the rematch could not have turned out any more different. What stayed the same was the AFC's Super Bowl representative. **Record: 16-2.**

Below: The Lamar Hunt Trophy frames Brady's winning smile following New England's AFC championship win in Pittsburgh.

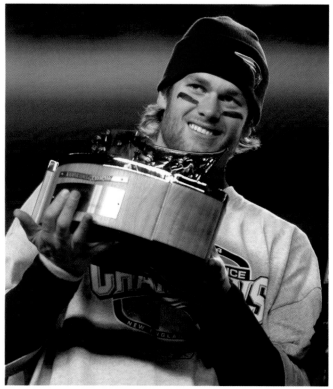

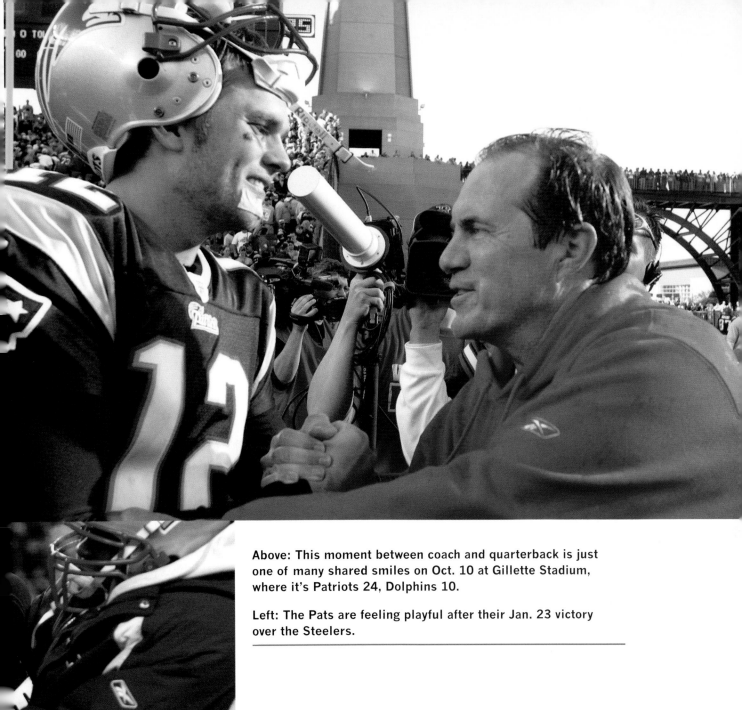

Above: This moment between coach and quarterback is just one of many shared smiles on Oct. 10 at Gillette Stadium, where it's Patriots 24, Dolphins 10.

Left: The Pats are feeling playful after their Jan. 23 victory over the Steelers.

SUPER BOWL XXXIX

Incomparable?

by DAN SHAUGHNESSY

February 6, 2005 | If Tom Brady were a politician he'd be John F. Kennedy — handsome, charming, and ever the winner. Making it to the top at a young age. The Camelot quarterback.

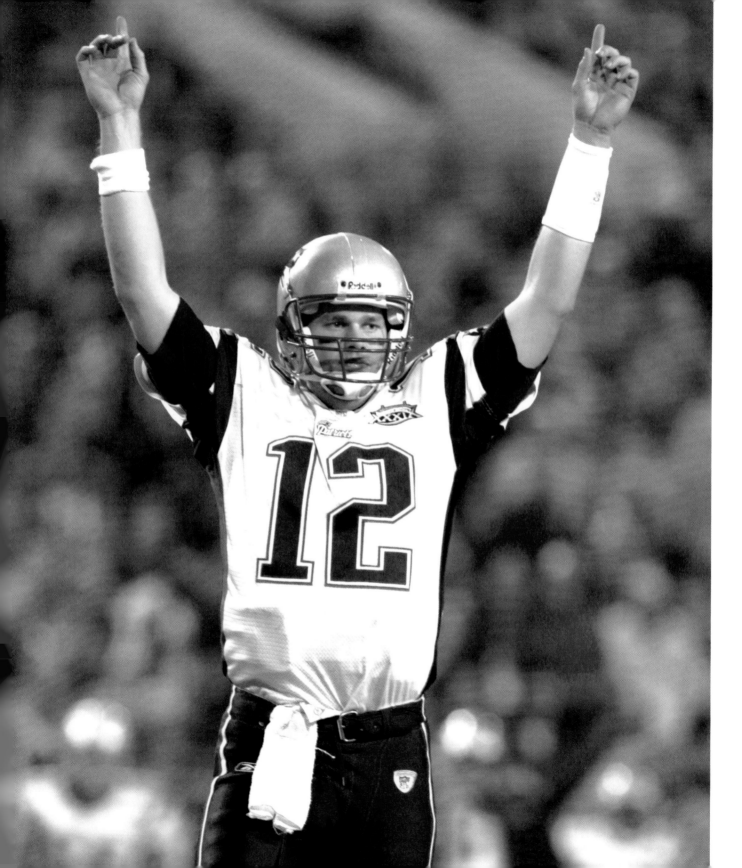

If he were a rock star he'd be Paul McCartney, the cute Beatle who was never a threat to parents. He'd compile a catalogue of eternally popular songs, all before the age of 28. Candlestick Park would be a special venue in his personal history.

If Tom Brady were a hockey player he'd be Bobby Orr, the boyish bachelor who owned Boston by his mid-20s. He'd be the coolest player on the ice, and half of the young fans in the building would wear his jersey. He'd be the best hockey player.

If he were a sitcom character he'd be Richie Cunningham, ever polite, always trying to do the right thing. He'd be the perfect son, and a great brother. He'd drink milkshakes and eat cheeseburgers with Ralph Malph and Potsie.

If he were a beverage he'd be a tall glass of cold milk. Wholesome. Healthy. Good for the bones and those dazzling white teeth.

If he were a college he'd be Stanford — cool, smart, West Coast, great reputation.

If he were a painting, he'd be Van Gogh's "Starry Night." All blues and yellows and gold stardust sprinkled across the canvas.

If he were a dog, he'd be a golden retriever. He'd be loyal, shiny, and athletic. He would never bark, but he'd make the children feel protected.

If Tom Brady were a basketball player he'd be Bill Russell. He would not have the arsenal of Wilt Chamberlain but he'd win the big matchup every time. He would not score a

WHAT'S ON TOM BRADY'S IPOD?

Here's the playlist he says he used in the locker room before Super Bowl XXXIX.

1. **Dream On,** Aerosmith
2. **Lose Yourself,** Eminem
3. **Possum Kingdom,** The Toadies
4. **If I Can't,** 50 Cent
5. **Fell on Black Days,** Soundgarden
6. **Bittersweet Symphony,** The Verve
7. **Award Tour,** A Tribe Called Quest
8. **Mysterious Ways,** U2
9. **I Can,** Nas
10. **Shiver,** Coldplay
11. **My Name Is,** Eminem
12. **I Still Haven't Found What I'm Looking For,** U2
13. **Jesus Walks,** Kanye West
14. **Beast of Burden,** Rolling Stones
15. **Wonderwall,** Oasis
16. **Black,** Pearl Jam
17. **Sunday Bloody Sunday,** U2
18. **Encore,** Jay-Z

Source: iTunes Music Store

lot of points, but he'd control the game. He'd make his teammates better. And he'd never choke down the stretch.

If he were a fruit he'd be an apple. He'd keep the doctor away. He'd be a good present to give your elementary school teacher. He'd be the best apple.

If he were a sportscaster he'd be Bob Costas. He'd be likeable, informed, quick-witted, and pleasant to watch. He'd never panic. He'd be able to hold down the anchor post no matter how much chaos was going on around him.

If he were a car he'd be an American-made four-door sedan with eight cylinders and whitewall tires. He'd be clean, but not too flashy. He'd have the horsepower to go fast, but most of the time he'd observe the speed limit.

If Tom Brady were a baseball player he'd be Derek Jeter. He'd emerge as a team leader at a young age and win many championship rings before turning 28. He'd have connections to the state of Michigan and he'd be good to his parents and his teammates would love him instead of being jealous. They'd love him because they know he's tough and he's a winner.

If he were a holiday he'd be the Fourth of July. He'd be a warm summer night with the Boston Pops playing Sousa's "Stars & Stripes Forever" while church bells peal.

If he were ice cream he'd be vanilla. With a cherry on top.

If Tom Brady were a tennis player he'd be

The Camelot quarterback, shiny and loyal as a golden retriever.

Arthur Ashe. He'd be brave and cool under pressure and he'd win championships even without the strongest game.

If he were a city he'd be San Diego, with perfect weather, beautiful beaches, and deep blue ocean waters.

If he were a state he'd be Montana. You know why.

If he were a movie star he'd be Matt Damon — modest, mindful of his roots, able to stay grounded in a starstruck environment, and smiling sheepishly when the compliments get too thick.

If Tom Brady were an NFL quarterback he'd be 8-0 in the playoffs with two Super Bowl MVP trophies in his house. He'd be leading his team into its third Super Bowl in four years. He'd be in Jacksonville preparing for the next biggest game of his life, against the Philadelphia Eagles.

If Tom Brady were quarterback of the New England Patriots there would be no doubt back in New England that the Patriots were going to win tonight. ♦

The Best

by DAN SHAUGHNESSY

February 7, 2005 | It's official.

Tom Brady follows Joe Montana into the football Hall of Fame. The University of Belichick takes its rightful place alongside Harvard and MIT. And the New England Patriots of the 21st century are established as an NFL dynasty on a par with the Packers of the 1960s, the Steelers of the '70s, the 49ers of the '80s, and the Cowboys of the '90s.

The Patriots last night won their second consecutive Super Bowl, and their third in four years, beating the Philadelphia Eagles, 24-21, by the banks of the St. Johns River. In front of 78,125 at Alltel Stadium and 800 million watching worldwide, Brady connected on 23 of 33 passes for 236 yards and two touchdowns and Deion Branch copped the MVP award with 11 catches for 133 yards.

The legend grows. Brady goes to 9-0 lifetime in the postseason, Bill Belichick moves ahead of Vince Lombardi with a playoff record of 10-1, Sam Adams gets bragging rights over Ben Franklin, and the Patriots are a gaudy 32-2 since Sept. 28, 2003. The Patriots tied a Packers record with their ninth consecutive playoff win. New England's stretch of domination includes an NFL-record 21-game winning streak, and a model of selflessness and teamwork for any coach who ever lived.

"Perhaps this one is more special," said Patriots linebacker Tedy Bruschi. "This shows everyone what kind of team we are and what kind of players we have to achieve this. People are going to have to start saying, 'These guys are one of the better teams in history.'"

"We're a title city," boasted Boston mayor Tom Menino, as he stood on the confetti-littered field moments after the game ended.

Heady times indeed. Years from now, it will be difficult to explain exactly what went on in New England sports during the golden days at the beginning of the 21st century. Who will believe that Greater Boston ruled the worlds of baseball and football simultaneously?

It's true. One hundred and two days after the Red Sox ended an 86-year drought in St. Louis, the sons of Belichick submitted another clutch performance in the ultimate game. Corey Dillon ran for 75 yards on 18 carries, including the go-ahead touchdown, and Branch caught everything thrown his way. New England's veteran smashmouth defense did the rest, rattling Philadelphia quarterback Donovan McNabb and forcing four Eagles turnovers. Patriots captain and spiritual leader Rodney Harrison sealed the victory with an interception of a desperation McNabb heave just before the clock expired.

Holding the Lombardi Trophy, Patriots owner Bob Kraft said, "To the fans of New England — the best fans that any team could wish for. This is your third Super Bowl in four years. This great accomplishment happened because we are blessed to have smart players and a brilliant coach in Bill Belichick and a great personnel department led by Scott Pioli... I'm proud that we won stressing team and not individual accomplishment."

Taking the stage after Kraft, Belichick told the crowd, "This trophy belongs to these players. They played great all year, played their best in the big games, and they deserve it."

The Patriots were far from perfect. It was 0-0 after one quarter, 7-7 at halftime, and 14-14 after three quarters. But New England wore down the Eagles' defense in the final quarter, scoring the go-ahead touchdown on a 2-yard run by Dillon at the beginning of the fourth, then making it 24-14 on a 22-yard Adam Vinatieri field goal with 8:40 left.

New England appeared to clinch the win with a Bruschi interception on the Eagles'

Time for confetti showers and waving the three-pete sign, as the victory parade winds through downtown Boston and Deion Branch gets it all on tape.

TOP 10

ensuing possession, but McNabb connected with Greg Lewis for a 30-yard TD with 1:48 left and the Eagles got the ball one more time. With 46 seconds left, the Patriots pinned the Eagles on their 4-yard line on a nifty punt by Josh Miller, and Harrison's interception ended it.

"For us to finish it off defensively, that was nice," said Bruschi. "It was nice Adam didn't have to go out there again with the game on the line."

"The Eagles were tough," Brady said while he walked toward the interview room. "But we had the determination. We fought hard for 60 minutes and came out the champs. It really hasn't sunk in yet and I don't think it's going

to sink in for a while."

Brady played the game with a heavy heart. His 94-year-old grandmother passed away during the week and he was more subdued than usual. On the field, though, he was his usual calm, commanding self.

It was 59 degrees at game time, better than Foxborough in February, but not quite dome-warm. In keeping with tradition established in 2002 in New Orleans, the Patriots came out of the smoke-filled tunnel en masse, wearing their white jerseys. Veterans Troy Brown, Vinatieri, and Christian Fauria fronted the first wave of defending champs. The Eagles followed the Patriots onto the field and it was immediately apparent that Philadelphia fans outnumbered those from New England.

After an All-American pregame celebration, which featured former presidents Clinton and Bush, the captains gathered at midfield for the ceremonial coin toss. Harrison called heads for the Patriots, the coin landed tails, and the Eagles naturally elected to receive.

Terrell Owens, who broke his right leg and tore ankle ligaments Dec. 19, was on the field for the Eagles' first series and caught a pass for 7 yards on the Eagles' second play from scrimmage. Owens went on to make nine catches for 122 yards in Philadelphia's defeat.

Philadelphia took a 7-0 lead in the fifth minute of the second quarter. The big play was a 40-yard completion over the middle to Todd Pinkston, who made a tremendous leaping catch ('scuse me while I kiss the sky). The nine-play, 81-yard drive was capped with a 6-yard TD pass from McNabb (who had too much time to throw) to L.J. Smith. At that juncture, the Eagles had nine first downs to New England's one.

The Patriots did not trail in many games in 2004-05. "Down 7-0 in a Super Bowl, sometimes you might get tight," said Bruschi. "But we've been in the big games."

Brady found David Givens in the right corner for a 4-yard touchdown pass to complete a 37-yard drive and make it 7-7. Givens

entertained 800 million watchers with a little T.O.-style celebration. Before halftime, Eugene Wilson broke his arm on kick return coverage, further depleting the Patriot secondary.

Brady surgically dissected the Eagles in the opening drive of the second half, taking the Patriots 69 yards on nine plays, capping the drive with a 2-yard TD toss to linebacker Mike Vrabel (seen that before?) for a 14-7 lead.

The Eagles were not dead. McNabb took advantage of the Patriots' impaired defensive backfield and took Philadelphia 74 yards in 10 plays. When McNabb hit Brian Westbrook over the middle for a 10-yard TD strike, it was 14-14 with 3:35 left in the third.

It was still tied when the third quarter ended (the first Super Bowl tied after three), but the Patriots were driving. With Dillon and Kevin Faulk grinding out yardage, the Patriots rolled to the Eagle 2-yard line, finally scoring from there on a run by Dillon. It was 21-14 with 13:44 left. The Patriots never trailed again. And now they've won three Super Bowls in four years, something that's only been done once (Cowboys in 1992, '94, '95) in the history of the NFL. ♦

Branch may be the MVP this time around, but Brady has possession of the Lombardi Trophy, and it looks as though he's threatening a good-natured game of keep away.

SUPER BOWL XXX

Simply Awesome

by BOB RYAN

February 7, 2005 | Could there possibly be any more doubts?

The best team in football has just concluded a grueling three-week exam period in which it faced three completely different challenges from three very good football teams. You can make a case — in fact, I'm going to — that this was the most difficult postseason task ever presented to a team attempting to win a Super Bowl.

The grades? A-plus, A-plus, and A-minus. The scores? 20-3, 41-27, and, finally, 24-21. Yup, for the third time in four years the Patriots have become the champions of the known football universe with a 3-point victory. But 3 or 30, it doesn't matter. The idea is to score more points than the other guys, and no team this century has found the weekly formula to do just that better than the New England Patriots.

Think about it: The New England Patriots are the unquestioned Team of the Century.

They are now in the enviable position of being able to judge championships. The first was, obviously, sweet. The second was vindicating and harrowing. But this one demanded a level of overall excellence that should make everyone involved feel incredibly proud. For what the Patriots have done in defeating these three particular teams in four weeks is nothing short of awe-inspiring.

"Indianapolis, we all know what kind of a team they are," said Bill Belichick. "Pittsburgh was the best team in the AFC all year. Philadelphia went wire-to-wire all year. I can't think of three tougher teams in my experience in the postseason."

This was a Patriots season unlike any other. After getting off to a 6-0 start, the entire season was threatened by the devastation of the secondary, forcing Belichick and his defensive staff to start improvising with players and schemes that made them the talk of both the NFL and the world of football in general. The brain trust had to make do with a converted wide receiver, a converted linebacker, and assorted people from the waiver wire. They kept winning and they made it look easy.

It was not.

The secondary nightmare continued right through last night, when starting free safety Eugene Wilson broke his arm while performing special teams duty late in the second quarter. This vaulted rookie Dexter Reid, a fourth-round pick from North Carolina, into the lineup. Were there scary moments? Oh, yes. Greg Lewis beat him for a touchdown pass in the fourth period, but the only thing that mattered was that he wasn't beaten more. He was good enough to get the job done, and on this team, Getting The Job Done is the only criterion for maintaining employment.

But it wasn't easy, and finding a way to compete with the personnel at hand may have been the toughest challenge of Belichick's coaching career.

"I can't say enough about these players," said Belichick. "These guys have worked so hard for the last six months. They just stepped up, kept working, kept fighting, and they did it again today."

This game was work. The Eagles came as advertised defensively, holding Tom Brady & Co. to one first down and no points in the first quarter. Brady looked curiously uncomfortable in the kind of Big Game that has made his reputation.

It didn't last, of course, because Tom Brady really is Mr. Cool, and it was only a matter of time before he and his mentor, Charlie Weis, found out what would and wouldn't work against an aggressive, speedy Philly defensive unit. With the typical Patriot lack of flamboyance, the offense calmly executed five excellent drives after falling behind, 7-0.

The first ended in frustration when Brady botched a handoff to Kevin Faulk and wound up fumbling the ball away after he had apparently recovered it. But three of the next four resulted in marches of 37, 69, and 66 yards for touchdowns and the following drive culminated in a 22-yard field goal by Adam Vinatieri that provided the Patriots with the eventual margin of victory.

We are used to seeing Brady do whatever is necessary to win. He is now 9-0 in three playoff visits. But Philadelphia defensive coordinator Jim Johnson apparently needs to see just a little more before he becomes a true Brady admirer. "Brady is on his way to being one of the better quarterbacks," he noted.

Thanks, coach. We'll keep our eye on him.

All week long, people peppered Belichick with questions about whether a third Super Bowl championship in four years would constitute a dynasty, and all week long he responded to such queries with the verbal equivalent of a stiff-arm. Naturally, people wanted to know if he would care to comment

> We are used to seeing Brady do whatever is necessary to win. He is now 9-0 in three playoff visits.

on that possibility now.

"We don't look at it that way," he explained. "We didn't look at it that way two days ago and we don't look at it that way now. We started out like everyone else — at the bottom of the mountain, and now we're at the top. When next season starts we'll start out at the bottom again."

Well, coach, how do these championships differ?

"If it's a scale of one to 10," he said, "they're all tens."

This season has to go down as an 11. The Patriots went 14-2 in the regular season, with the Pittsburgh loss loaded with asterisks and the second Miami game a complete giveaway. And leave it to Belichick to point out that "we also beat both of those teams, so we can say we took [on] and defeated all comers."

They also peaked at precisely the right time, playing brilliant all-around games against the Colts and Steelers and then probing and adjusting against the Eagles until getting the thing calibrated just so.

We can get started with the historical judgments in due time. Right now all that needs to be said is that the Patriots once again met every challenge and are — how great does this sound? — the Team of the Century.

Leave early for a good spot at the parade. ◆

Wintry weather has never stopped Pats fans from celebrating a Super Bowl victory in Boston, where champions seem to enjoy parading by in duck boats.

V-Day

by DAN SHAUGHNESSY

February 9, 2005 | Letter to Vince Lombardi, now coaching in a place where the Hail Mary passes are completed every day:

Dear Vince,

I hope that it's OK to call you Vince. I know we never met, but I read Jerry Kramer's book ("Instant Replay") when I was a kid and I watched the Ice Bowl from my warm den when I was in middle school.

Anyway, I'm writing to tell you about this pro football team we have here in New England. I know you've probably been paying attention from your luxury box in the sky, but there are things you should know about these guys. Maybe you're getting tired of hearing about how Bill Belichick is a genius and has a 10-1 playoff record. People keep talking about how he's topped your postseason record of 9-1, but don't be annoyed because Belichick isn't having anything to do with the phony comparison. He reminds everyone that you won five NFL Championships. He knows the reason you won only two Super Bowls is because they didn't invent the ultimate game until the end of your reign with the Packers. We all know that.

Maybe you're a little sick of the rampant "dynasty" talk that's spread across America since the Patriots won. That's understandable. But the NFL has lowered its "dynasty" standards since you coached in the league. It's tougher now because of a thing called the salary cap and the NFL's obsession with parity. The league today legislates to avoid the kind of dominance that marked your years in Green Bay.

Trust me when I tell you that you'd love this Patriots team, and you'd be OK with comparisons to your Packers of the 1960s. You know why? Because they're old school, that's why. And I'm not just talking old school, NFL-style. I'm talking old school, Fordham-style. Boola boola, raccoon coats, leather helmets, win one for the Gipper. Old-school old school.

Obviously, you know how tough it can be to coach professional ballplayers. And you know it was only getting tougher when you retired from the game. I'm sure it's been sad for you to watch the degeneration of team play in the decades since you left us. Big money, loss of fundamentals, and something called ESPN conspired to create a generation of athletes many of whom are more interested in self-promotion than winning. Coaches lost the hammer somewhere along the way and it's become difficult to get your players to do what you want them to do.

George Bush welcomes the three-time Super Bowl champion Patriots back to the White House in 2005.

That's why you'd love the Patriots, Vince. Really. They've got a 33-year-old career wide receiver who played defensive back most of this year. They've got a young all-pro defensive lineman who plays fullback and blocks for Corey Dillon in goal-line situations. They've got a veteran linebacker who's caught touchdown passes in two Super Bowls. Two-way players, Coach. And they do it willingly. How's that for old school?

The quarterback would remind you a little of Bart Starr. Remember how Unitas and Y.A. Tittle put up all the gaudy numbers while Bart was content to win those championships? It's like that now. This kid Tom Brady gets ignored while folks talk about Peyton Manning and Michael Vick. Like Starr, Brady completes the short passes, makes few mistakes, and wins games just about every week. He's also humble like Bart. He deflects the attention. I know most everybody did that back in your day, but believe me, it's rare now.

It's been like this for a while, Coach. These Patriots won 21 straight games in one stretch. They won nine straight playoff games. They won in brutally cold weather, just like your guys. They won the close ones and they won the blowouts.

Like your players in Green Bay, these Patriots immersed themselves in the local community. They've earned the unconditional love of their fans and returned that love.

You've been gone for 25 years, but the spirit never died in Green Bay. There are still thousands of fans in Wisconsin who share stories of the glory days, when you and your players were the kings of the NFL.

That's what it's like in New England now. These are our glory days, and 40 years from today we'll be spinning the tall tales of a coach named Belichick, a quarterback named Brady, and a band of gridiron brothers who dominated the NFL and demonstrated the true meaning of the word "team."

NOW WHAT?

New Challenges

by JACKIE MACMULLAN

May 29, 2005 | The money can change everything **if you are not careful. It heightens expectations that have already reached Herculean proportions. It engenders envy, jealousy, and resentment. If nothing else, it guarantees you will pick up every single check, if you haven't done that already, for the rest of your playing days.**

Tom Brady was already famous, and successful beyond his dreams. Now he has the money to go with it. His latest six-year, $60 million contract rightfully puts him among the highest-paid players in sports, and while NFL contracts aren't guaranteed, the $14.5 million signing bonus is money in the bank.

This deal was a no-brainer. Brady is the one player the Patriots cannot do without. He's a once-in-a-lifetime franchise quarterback with the poise and polish and resume to command a "sign-at-all-costs" approach.

Of course, clearing the necessary cash for Brady has its downside. It doesn't quite leave enough to go around for everyone else looking for a lucrative payday. Is that why, in the end, New England couldn't or wouldn't go the extra step with offensive lineman Joe Andruzzi? Not necessarily. The team placed a value on Andruzzi and determined it would not venture beyond that. But is that value influenced by the spreadsheet of the entire team, and the

These days, Brady can afford to take it easy at his team's annual charity golf tournament.

need to make sure it is enough to lock up its star quarterback? Probably.

It's not as simple as giving Brady less to pay Andruzzi more, but you can be sure somebody will cite that theory the first time Brady throws a couple of picks or gets flattened at the line of scrimmage.

Brady learned after the fact that Andruzzi had signed with Cleveland. They've talked numerous times since, and the quarterback still feels the sting of losing the veteran lineman.

"I was listening to Joe's brother on the ra-

dio," Brady said. "It was tough to hear him talk about how much Joe loved the Patriots and how much he really wanted to be here. That's hard, especially since I had a relationship with Joe, his brothers, his wife, his mother and father. I hope and expect we'll be friends for a long time."

The disappointment is clear in Brady's voice, yet his measured comments lack the raw emotion that spilled over when his close friend, Lawyer Milloy, was released days before the season opener in 2003. Back then,

Brady struck a tone of defiance that was appreciated by his teammates but frowned upon by the front office.

"In some ways, as I'm growing, and seeing it more often, I've become more accustomed to those things," Brady explained. "It happens. You watch something as crazy as Jerry Rice. I think it's great for Jerry Rice that Denver signed him. You say, 'What about your legacy, Jerry?' and he says, 'I never played for that. I played for fun.' He played all those years in San Francisco, then he went to the Raiders, and his time was up there, and then he went to Seattle, and his time was up there, and now it's Denver.

"I don't know. I think it's special to play for one team."

Even though Brady remains in a Patriots uniform, he knows he will not be playing for the same team in 2005. He laments the departure of defensive coordinator Romeo Crennel and his offensive guru, Charlie Weis. He understands there will be a huge void both on the field and in the locker room if linebacker Tedy Bruschi cannot play this season. Andruzzi is gone. Ty Law is gone. Roman Phifer is gone. Each contributed greatly to the fabric of the team.

"This will be our most challenging year," Brady predicted. "It's up to us to see this team develop into however it morphs into.

"You want it to be at a championship level. My job as the quarterback is to make sure not that we're better than last year, but that we are the best we can be this year."

Without Weis pushing him, challenging him, and, in some cases, berating him, Brady will assume an even larger chunk of the offensive responsibility.

"It was different without Charlie at the passing camp," Brady conceded. "Charlie was such a big personality. He ran the show. The other guys are very capable, but it's

> "I don't know. I think it's special to play for one team."

just a matter of how fast we'll all progress together.

"I learned so much from Charlie. I carry that with me. His approach to the game, to the meeting room, practice, how he prepared the day of the game, I've learned so much from that. I'm going to lose some but hopefully not all of that."

A recent passing camp enabled Brady to spend some time with newly signed backup Doug Flutie, the local legend who always seems to find his way onto the field.

"We talked about the fact when he was graduating high school, I was 4 years old," Brady said. "He's a great guy. I really enjoyed him. He's 42 years old, but he acts like he's 10."

If Flutie does play, it will mean one of two things: either the team is winning (or losing) big, or Brady is hurt. The latter scenario is a taboo subject, like talking about a no-hitter while it's in progress. Brady has been remarkably injury-free. He is the heartbeat of this team, the only player who was able to take the big money and stay. That was not an option for Andruzzi, Law, Milloy, Damien Woody, and others.

Again, the money is tricky.

"Every year we deal with it. You try to get the best deal you can, but you also know it's going to affect your teammates," the quarterback admitted.

Brady vows to be a Patriot lifer. His contract is structured accordingly. Asked what he's done with his newfound riches, the quarterback answered, "I haven't bought a thing. I made more my first year than I ever thought possible in my wildest dreams.

"When you are a kid, everyone wants to grow up and play sports. You want to succeed. But there are still times when I sit around with my mom and dad and say, 'Can you believe this?'"

Three Super Bowl wins later, yes, we absolutely can. ◆

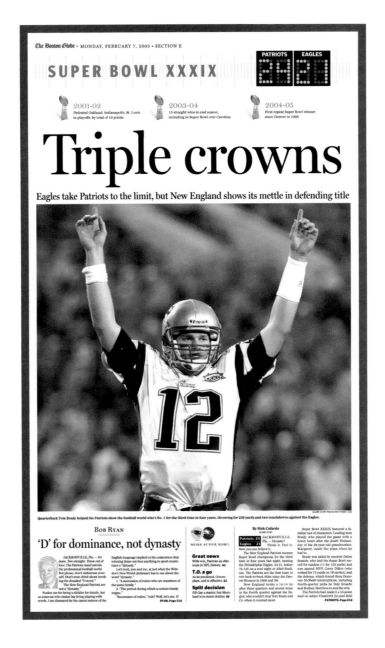